# RUN FOR YOUR LIFE

# RUN FOR YOUR LIFE

## THE REMARKABLE TRUE STORY OF A FAMILY FORCED INTO HIDING AFTER LEAKING RUSSIAN SECRETS

# SUE WILLIAMS

SIMON &
SCHUSTER

London · New York · Sydney · Toronto · New Delhi

RUN FOR YOUR LIFE
First published in Australia in 2024 by
Simon & Schuster (Australia) Pty Limited
Suite 19A, Level 1, Building C, 450 Miller Street, Cammeray, NSW 2062

10 9 8 7 6 5 4 3 2 1

Simon & Schuster: Celebrating 100 Years of Publishing in 2024.
Sydney New York London Toronto New Delhi
Visit our website at www.simonandschuster.com.au

A catalogue record for this
book is available from the
NATIONAL LIBRARY OF AUSTRALIA  National Library of Australia

ISBN: 9781761427961

Cover design: Luke Causby/Blue Cork
Front cover images: Unsplash; Luke Causby/Blue Cork
Back cover images: Nick Stride
Typeset by Midland Typesetters, Australia
Printed and bound by CPI Group (UK) Ltd, Croydon
CR0 4YY

MIX
Paper | Supporting
responsible forestry
FSC
www.fsc.org   FSC® C171272

To my son Michael, who carried himself with dignity, respect and maturity through incredibly challenging times, and to my daughter Anya, the strongest and most beautiful person in the world who, despite her struggles, always found a way.

— Nick Stride

# CONTENTS

# PROLOGUE

ON A RUGGED BEACH of fiery red sand, shark-infested waters and patrolling crocodiles somewhere in the remote reaches of Australia's far northwest, a little family are fighting the battle of their lives.

Penniless, they've fashioned spears from young saplings in the hope of catching a few fish and octopus in the rockpools to cook over their campfire with their last handful of rice, but they're rapidly running out of food, of water, and of hope.

They've been living for five months now like this, in absolute isolation on this curve of gritty sand under the relentless Kimberley sun, the last dregs of a total of three years hiding out off the grid on the furthest frontiers of the lonely Dampier Peninsula. But now the ragged, barefoot family of four – British man Nick Stride, his Russian wife Luda, their son Michael, aged 17, and daughter Anya, 16 – realise they can't survive like this for much longer.

They've been on the run for over seven years from one of the most powerful men in Russia, the one-time deputy of Vladimir Putin, and for three of those years also from the immigration authorities in

1

Australia who refused to help them after they fled to the other side of the world to seek asylum. Now, however, they know their time as fugitives must be coming to an end.

'It was all becoming too much,' Nick says. 'It was so, so hard living like that. By then, we were all absolutely as tough as nails, but we were starting to crack under the pressure. I think a lot of people might have died in that situation. And I knew we well might if it went on.'

Along the way, the tight foursome has battled crocodiles, sharks, snakes and deadly spiders, and survived cyclones and bushfires that raced across the land with a speed and fury that destroyed everything in their path. They've been stranded at sea on a tiny dinghy with a broken engine, drifting into ever-deeper waters; stuck in a quagmire of sand in battered vehicles; and forced to wade through waist-deep floods when the monsoonal rains broke.

Now, in threadbare clothes and with their skin stained a deep red from the pindan dust, so fine it has seeped through everything, they are ready to give up, close to the very end of their limits.

And then, one day, a man drives from seemingly nowhere onto their beach. They're startled. The reason they chose this place was that it's so out of the way, no one ever chances by. And the man looks back at them, plainly shocked too to see other human life in such a spot.

'Hello there!' he eventually calls, approaching them, realising from their dishevelled appearance that there must be something terribly wrong. 'Are you all right?'

Nick tries to force a smile and keep his voice from trembling. 'Yes, mate,' he replies, not wanting to raise suspicion. 'We're fine, thanks.'

The man looks doubtful. 'Hey,' he says, looking at the family's dog, Molly. 'I've got a bit of chicken here for your dog.' He tosses a couple of chicken wings, still with plenty of meat attached, to the ground and Molly pounces on them. The family stand transfixed.

'We were open-mouthed at the sight of chicken, and of our dog eating it,' Nick recounts, later. 'We were all thinking, *We could have eaten that*. It looked so good. We were all close to starving, but suddenly, Molly is eating better than any of us!'

The man notices their distraught expressions, and coughs politely to attract their attention. 'Actually,' he says, 'I've got some beefburgers in the truck. Would you like some?'

The family stare at him in disbelief, as if he's just offered them the keys to the kingdom of heaven.

'The taste of meat after so long, it was incredible,' Nick says. 'It was then I realised we couldn't go on like this any longer. Everything, and everyone, was falling apart. We'd been through so much up to that point, but I knew, however nervous I'd been of the threats from the Russians, and then of our family being split up and deported to different countries by the Australian immigration authorities, this was turning into a living death. We had to get out.'

And he wonders, not for the first time, how the hell his and his family's lives have gone so catastrophically wrong.

3

# PART ONE

# TO RUSSIA WITHOUT LOVE

# ONE

# TO RUSSIA WITHOUT LOVE

**HE'D LOST HIS WIFE**, his two children and most of his will to live when that fateful call came through with the offer of a job in Russia. Construction worker Nick Stride was taken aback. He knew nothing about the country, beyond what he'd seen in James Bond movies, but it sounded like a great adventure, and the money was good. Besides, he was keen to get away from everything at home. His life was a mess and every attempt to fix it had failed. He was desperate for a fresh start in a new place, far away from everything, and everyone, he knew in the UK.

'Yes, I'll take it,' he said down the phone to his old boss at the glazing company where he'd once worked. His boss was surprised. Nick hadn't even asked what it was he'd be doing, or in what part of the massive nation he'd be located. 'I didn't really care,' Nick says now. 'I just wanted to get out and go somewhere new.'

To Nick, at that time, it felt like something of a lifeline. He'd married young, at twenty-one, in 1989 and, within the first few months, realised it was a terrible mistake. By then, however, his wife was pregnant and, having grown up with a mother and father who'd both suffered as a result of their parents' broken marriages, and feeling it was the only honourable path, he resolved to stick it out.

His son was a joy from the moment he was born, and his daughter, who came along less than a year later, was the apple of his eye. He'd never before felt so fulfilled. He doted on his children, even while he and his wife seemed to be growing apart. They wanted completely different things out of life and had little in common. He loved the great outdoors and yearned to travel and explore the world; she seemed perfectly content to stay in their city of Southampton in the south of England.

Their children were the glue that kept them together. Whenever Nick came home to the family's modest two-up, two-down house, his son and daughter would race to meet him at the door, and cling to his legs, until he'd pick them up, kiss them and then take them into the loungeroom to play. By now, his son was four years old and into everything, and his daughter was a gorgeous, bright little three-year-old. Most evenings, he'd play and read to the children and see them fed and bathed before they went to bed, and then either sit with a book or watch TV.

But one day in late 1993 when he came home from work, expecting his kids to come scurrying to meet him, the door opened to an empty corridor. As he closed it behind him, he heard an echo he'd never noticed before. The house was strangely, disturbingly silent, and his heart lurched. A sudden thought hit him, and he sprinted into each of the children's bedrooms – to find most of their clothes and their toys gone. He raced into his bedroom, and it, too, had been stripped. Frantic, he rang every one of her friends he could think of, but no one seemed to know what had happened, or where his family might have gone. His wife had left no trace.

Nick contacted the police but back then, in 1994, they said there wasn't much they could do. There was no sign of foul play, it was unlikely any crime had been committed and, as such, it was a personal matter between Nick and his wife. 'But my children,' he implored them. 'How can I find my children?' The officer looked back at him with obvious sympathy but shrugged his shoulders. They weren't willing to get involved. Nick was devastated. He'd grown up with a strong sense of right and wrong, and this was obviously so wrong, but there appeared to be little he could do.

Over the next few months, Nick visited every school in the south of England, searching for his son and daughter, but they were nowhere to be found. No Strides had been registered at any of the schools, nor any children in his wife's maiden name. 'I was desperate,' he says. 'I went to every one of them, but nothing. I think by the end, I was starting to look a bit suspicious, lurking around so many schools. It's a wonder I didn't get arrested.'

Finally, in despair, he engaged a solicitor to see what could be done. It took three months, but eventually his wife and children were tracked down, and she was summoned to appear in court. Nick attended that day with his heart in his mouth, but neither she, nor the children, turned up. The court ruled in her absence, however, that Nick should have access to his children. It took many more months for a reunion to be arranged and to take place, and that day is seared forever on his memory.

'As soon as my son saw me, he came running to me, just like he used to,' Nick says, tears in his eyes. 'My daughter was more hesitant, shyer. But when it was time to go, my son grabbed me around the neck and clung to me and wouldn't let me go. They had to pull him off me. He was crying and I was crying and all the social workers who'd organised the meeting were crying. It was horrendous. And then, suddenly, it was all over. And I realised that this was an impossible situation, and I would probably never see them again.'

Back in the empty house that evening, Nick felt so devastated he considered taking his own life. 'I was in so much pain,' he says. 'It was incredible. I absolutely doted on those kids. They were every-thing to me . . . I was absolutely convinced I'd never see them again, and I didn't know how I could ever cope with that.'

Salvation came, however, from the most unlikely source: an old schoolfriend, Kev, who'd kept in contact with him over the eight years since they'd both left. When they next met up for a drink and a chat, it seemed Kev could see the anguish on his mate's face and sense his hopelessness in the way he sat slumped at the table over his untouched beer.

Not knowing what else to do, Kev came up with a suggestion straight out of left field. 'Look, mate, I can't bear to see you like this,' he said. 'You need to get yourself together. How about a trip, the two of us, to . . . Australia?'

Nick looked up, shocked. Kev looked back at him, also seem-ingly surprised at his own suggestion. 'Really?' Nick asked.

Kev recovered himself quickly, though Nick could see he was putting on a brave face. 'Yes, really,' he replied. 'Let's do it!'

Nick pondered it for a few moments, then asked, 'Do you have any money?'

Kev looked uncomfortable. 'Well, no, not really.'

'Oh, bugger it,' said Nick. 'I've got some. I'll buy two tickets.'

That night when Nick went home, he wrote a list of the ten things he wanted to do that year, with diving with sharks on the Great Barrier Reef at number one. 'They were all things I'd normally be too scared to do,' he says. 'But I remember saying to myself, "Right, now I can do whatever I want without fear, because I've already faced the very worst thing that could ever happen to me".'

The next morning, Nick went straight to a travel agent and booked two return tickets on Royal Brunei Airlines from London to Darwin for himself and Kev for their two-week adventure. They left just a few days later.

Darwin was a shock to them both. Hot and sticky and lush and tropical, it was a jarring contrast to life in one of Britain's biggest – and greyest – port cities. Every day was gloriously sunny and warm, everyone seemed cheerful and friendly, and the population was a vibrant mix of what seemed like happy-go-lucky people from all parts of the world. With less than half the number of inhabitants of their hometown, and spread over an area forty-four times bigger, it still felt very much like a knockabout hillbilly town. The main thoroughfare, Mitchell Street, was lined with rowdy bars and restaurants, where dusty, sunburnt locals and visitors drank as if their lives depended on it. But they were all very welcoming, even if fights did sometimes spill over onto the street outside.

On his first day in Darwin, Nick tore up the return part of his ticket, thinking he never wanted to return to England. But Kev was the opposite. He hated every minute of being there. The pair did the main sights together: walking along the waterfront lapped by the aquamarine Timor Sea; checking out the elegant Supreme Court and cyclone-battered Government House buildings; wandering through the landscaped greenery of Bicentennial Park; fish-feeding down at Doctor's Gully; and then eating freshly caught fish at the old wooden Darwin Wharf. Nick was eager to see, and do, as much as he could, to stop his mind wandering back to his children and to the despair that he always felt when he pictured them. One day, he'd tell them about this, he mused. And maybe one day, he'd do it all again – and with them this time.

Further afield, he and Kev went swimming at crocodile-free Howard Springs National Park and watched the saltwater crocs on the Adelaide River jumping to snap up meat dangled from the end of poles. Then, on the Thursday night of the weekly Mindil Beach market, they bought food from the myriad Asian food stalls clustered on the seafront and sat on the sand, eating out of cardboard boxes, as they watched the fierce oranges, reds and yellows of the sun setting over the water.

'Can you imagine anything better than this?' Nick would ask Kev.

His mate would shrug. 'What I'd give now for sausage and chips,' he'd reply. 'And a decent pint. And a beach where everything's not trying to kill you.'

At night, the pair would go out drinking, play pool and chat to the locals, while telling each other how much – or how little – they missed home. Kev trumpeted Southampton for many things – being the original departure points for the *Mayflower* in 1620 when the Pilgrims set out for America, and of the *Titanic* almost three centuries later when it embarked on a similar, but much less successful, voyage. Then there was its most famous comedy export, Benny Hill. Nick remained unmoved. They were all in the past; Australia promised so much for the future. But Kev was hopelessly homesick, and by the end of the two weeks, Nick was relieved to farewell his friend.

Though he'd fallen in love with Australia, he was fast running out of funds. People always seemed keen to offer him a helping hand, however. One woman he met in the bar of his hotel turned out to have her own cleaning company and said there was plenty of cleaning work around, if he didn't mind doing that. He didn't mind at all, and so spent some of his time cleaning houses at the navy base HMAS Coonawarra, a ten-minute walk from the city centre, and the rest at the army's new Robertson Barracks about fifteen kilometres out. The only downside lay in the officers inspecting the work.

'We'd go in and bleach the walls and clean the floors and take all the drawers out of cabinets and wipe all the runners,' Nick says. 'You'd be sure there wouldn't be any dust left, but then some army officer would come in and just pull everything apart. And if he found a speck of dust . . . all hell would break loose. But the money was enough to live on, to pay for accommodation, food, beer and entertainment.'

It was a good time to be in Australia, and Nick was starting to come around to the idea that he might never leave. John Howard was celebrating the end of his first year in office, and the economy was well out of the recession of the early 1990s. Inflation, interest rates and unemployment were all low, there was steady wages growth and plenty of confidence in the future. There were cuts in immigration, but the Government was talking about increasing the quota of skilled migrants, which would suit Nick fine, giving him an easy path to both work and residency.

The country seemed a vibrant, endlessly fascinating place to live. Ski instructor Stuart Diver had survived the Thredbo land-slide, politician Pauline Hanson was being caricatured as Pauline

Pantsdown, everyone was talking about a constitutional convention on the way to becoming a republic, actor Geoffrey Rush had won an Oscar for *Shine*, and a little movie made for $700,000 in eleven days, *The Castle*, was becoming a box office mega-hit. Tennis player Pat Rafter had won the US Open, sprinter Cathy Freeman had become the first Australian woman to win a title at the World Athletics Championships and the ingenious jail escapee dubbed the 'postcard bandit' by police was staging a series of daring bank robberies all over Australia.

'It just seemed a very fun, optimistic country and that's something I really appreciated,' Nick says. 'I still had dark days when I thought about my kids and I missed them so much, but I had to face the fact that I'd lost them, and I had to get on with my own life. Australia seemed like the perfect place to get away from all that misery and despair, but sometimes it would still catch up with me and overwhelm me.'

After two months of cleaning houses, Nick had a free afternoon and returned to his backpackers' lodge early for a swim. He started chatting to another man, Nathan, who asked him what he was doing and how long he was planning to stay. Nathan had a couple of motorbikes that he was looking to take down to Brisbane, some 3500 kilometres away, and asked Nick if he could ride a bike. Still game for adventure, Nick readily agreed to accompany him – especially as Nathan said he'd pay for a plane ticket for him back to Darwin afterwards.

It was a fabulous five days, with the pair stopping off along the way to see some of the route's best-known landmarks. They followed the trail through Kakadu to the mighty Jim Jim Falls, swam in the thermal springs, ate steak and chips in the classic 1930s outback Daly Waters Pub and explored the site of one of Australia's biggest gold rushes at Battery Hill by Tennant Creek. Then they turned east to cross into Queensland. When they hit Mt Isa, they drove up the city lookout for the 360-degree views of the town and its infamous smelter stacks, then roared off through the outback via Julia Creek, Richmond and Hughenden before making for the coast at Townsville.

'You've seen more of Australia than most Australians!' Nathan said to Nick. 'What do you think of it so far?'

Nick didn't hesitate. 'Marvellous!' he said. 'It's like another world. I love it.'

Queensland was so different to the Northern Territory, but Nick liked it just as much. This state felt like a permanent holiday destination because, for many Australians, it was. In Townsville, the pair took a snorkelling tour off the Great Barrier Reef, where Nick was amazed to see small reef sharks circling their boat.

'Diving with sharks, tick!' he said to Nathan, who looked confused. 'Only nine more to go.'

The pair rode on down the coast, often dazzled by the sun in their eyes, and the sight of the ocean and the golden beaches along the way. By the time they reached Brisbane, Nick had decided Queensland would be an even nicer place to live than the Northern Territory. He liked Brisbane instantly, too – a slick capital, small enough to be easily navigable, but large enough to lose yourself in. He loved all the great views of the glittering Brisbane River, and the cafes, restaurants, bars and music venues.

Again, he found the locals extremely friendly. One businesswoman he found himself chatting to one day in a bar said if he wanted to stay, she'd be happy to sponsor him through her company.

They became good mates and met up often at the weekends with her little boy. One day, they were sitting around at an outdoor bar, and someone nearby started teasing her son. He immediately ran over to Nick and jumped straight into his lap.

The woman looked surprised, then smiled. 'I thought you said you didn't have any children,' she admonished him.

'No, I don't,' he fibbed.

She shook her head. 'You lying bastard. I know you've got kids. My son would only go to someone he feels absolutely safe with. So I reckon you're a dad. How many?'

Nick knew when he'd been caught out and confessed he had two, but that he didn't see them anymore. At that, he felt the dark cloud coming down again until it engulfed him.

'So what do you plan to do?' she asked, gently.

'Well . . .' he started but then stopped abruptly.

'Tell me,' she urged.

'I have this list of ten things I want to do,' Nick finally confessed. 'I started with diving with sharks . . . '

'And when you've completed those ten things?'

Nick looked down into his beer and could feel his eyes start to water. By the time he looked up, the whole world had blurred. 'I didn't think much further than that,' he said. 'But maybe . . . when I've done them all . . . I'll just walk off into the outback and die.'

The woman put her hand on his shoulder. 'No, Nick,' she said. 'You can't do that, you can't think that way.'

'Why not?' Nick replied, despair in his voice. 'Without my kids, I've got nothing to live for.'

'Listen to me,' she said. 'What's your son going to do when one day he travels all the way to Australia and finds you've gone? What's it going to be like for your daughter to know her dad had given up on life? Nick, honestly, you can't be that selfish.'

That evening, back in his motel room, Nick thought about what she'd said. It made sense and it had jolted him, he couldn't lie. Maybe he was being selfish, wallowing in his own misery. What if one day his kids did try to find him? He'd hate to cause them any more pain and suffering.

The next morning, he woke up feeling a new lightness. He realised that he'd decided yes, he needed to start living again. That was Australia's gift. Now, after three and a half months away, he needed to go back to Britain, tie up loose ends, agree to file for divorce from his wife, try to see his kids again, and then work out what he should do with his life.

He flew back to Darwin the next day and went into the travel agent. There, they told him he still had a valid ticket back to the UK on their books, despite his having torn up his own copy.

Nick caught the first flight back that had an empty seat, full of optimism about rebuilding his life. Once he'd seen his wife and children, he planned to return to Australia, but knew that first he'd have to earn some serious money to make a new start possible. His plane landed at Heathrow on Christmas Eve, and he caught the train straight back to Southampton to stay at his older brother Andy's place. The day after Boxing Day, he started a new job at a glazing company.

It was still proving problematic to see his children, and Nick soon felt the familiar darkness descend. He wondered if he'd last even the minimum six months he knew it would take him to earn enough money to return to Australia.

And then his phone rang with the offer to go over to Russia to work. Nick leapt at the chance. He had no idea what it might involve, but he didn't care. It would mean leaving Britain and the bad memories behind, he'd earn a lot of money quickly and he'd be well placed either to return to Australia or try somewhere new.

'I was excited by the thought,' Nick says. 'I thought it was such a lucky break. It was exciting. What could possibly go wrong?'

# TWO

# A STRANGER IN MOSCOW

ARRIVING IN MOSCOW IN March 1998 felt, to Nick, like landing on another planet. The weather was cold and wet and just as grey as it had been back home in England, but the people wore drab clothing, the buildings en route from the airport looked grim and depressingly utilitarian, and the traffic was horrendous.

Nothing, however, could dampen his spirits. He was somewhere new and exotic, and for someone whose favourite reading, as a boy, had been poring over the family atlas, it felt like the biggest adventure of his life.

'I'd tried to do some research before I left but it had been impossible to get any concrete picture of what it was going to be like,' he says. 'The company had painted a Cold War kind of image. They'd told us to take cigarettes out there with us to barter for food – which turned out to be completely wrong – so they didn't have much of an idea either.

'The only things we all knew about Russia were from James Bond movies, and the villains were nearly always Russian. There's never a good Russian. But I was excited to be there and away from Britain. I'd briefed a lawyer about a divorce so that would be sorted out while I was away, and I just wanted to go for it and start on a new life.'

Nick, along with the other nineteen workers from the company, were on a mission to help build a new British Embassy in Moscow. They were picked up from the airport in a van and driven for two hours through dense traffic straight to the site, in the upmarket Arbat District in the city's historical centre. As a construction glazier – a glazier who specialises in the delicate work of constructing free-standing glass walls – Nick had expert skills that were in high demand, as well as something even rarer among the team working there: no criminal record. As a result, at the meeting with British security that took place immediately on site, Nick was told he'd been appointed a supervisor and one of a select group of four of the men who'd just arrived who would have access to the highly restricted inner core of the embassy.

The security briefing was thorough and not a little daunting. If they were one of the few to be permitted inside the Chancery, they had to be aware that they'd be working in close quarters with highly classified documents that Russian intelligence would love to have access to. As a result, they might well be regularly photographed coming and going by agents from the Federal Security Service (FSB) of the Russian Federation – the successor to the former Soviet Union's KGB. It was possible they'd be approached by them too as potential leakers of information, and they should be wary of any locals trying to befriend them, or even chat, when they were out and about. In fact, they should avoid socialising with Russians, full stop. Of course, the Cold War was in the past, but who knew what might happen in the future?

The security chief said that many expat workers routinely ended up with Russian girlfriends, and they weren't in a position to stop that, but he stressed that anyone becoming romantically involved should bring their girlfriend's passport to the embassy to be checked. It was common practice for any intelligence service to set 'honeypot' traps for foreign workers. It was likely as well that the FSB would enter their apartments when they weren't home, looking for documents, although they'd leave no trace so no one would ever know they'd been. And, importantly, whenever any high-ranking Russian officials came into the area in their motorcade of black cars, flanked by police cars and motorcyclists, no one was ever to take a photo. It was rumoured that someone had once tried . . . and been shot for their trouble.

Then the group was divided into threes – Nick was paired with his mate Nolan and another Kev – and driven to the apartments that had been allocated for them. 'It was organised by a Russian company,' Nick says. 'They determined where we stayed and how much we paid. We were paying US$750 a month, where normally an apartment like ours, a bare little place with a basic cooker and no washing machine in a four-storey block, would be less than US$60. There was a grandmother living there with her adult children and, at first, they said the grandmother would have to stay and share with us. We immediately said, Sorry, we didn't think she'd fit in. It was very strange. But it was just so interesting to be there and be learning about the country and how it worked from the inside.'

While the work was demanding and entailed long hours, Nick quickly began to enjoy both the challenges of being engaged in such a prestigious project, and his time off. The men who'd come over with him were mostly heavy drinkers and regarded their time in Moscow as an opportunity to earn good money and go wild in a place far from home that sometimes seemed to revolve around the ready availability of cheap alcohol. Their nights out inevitably ended up in huge fights with the locals or other foreign workers.

'It was a pretty wild place,' says Nick. 'I'd never drunk much and I didn't over there either, so I ended up avoiding a lot of the English nightmare. They'd go to the pubs all the time, drink like fish and then you could feel in the air that things were about to kick off. Then they'd have these huge punch-ups – that was their idea of a good night out. They ended up barred from most of the bars in Moscow but there was one bar they went to all the time that was owned by a local mafia group that loved them as they spent so much money there. That group gave them protection and if any Russians or Finns started amping up, they'd be taken out the back and given a good kicking.

'It was just such a crazy time, and it was like there were no laws that applied. Some people would get arrested but then just bribe their way out of trouble. One night, a lot of the lads were fighting Russians from the Militsiya – like the traffic police and detectives – in a bar and it became such a scrum, the military police turned up. They were all armed with rifles, but the English were still fighting them. They eventually all got arrested but when they didn't turn up for work the next day, the foreman went down to the station, paid money and got them all out again. So, I'd do my best to avoid them and I'd just go out with Nolan or Kev to different clubs to see what they were like, and relax and try to find out more about the Russian way of life.'

Communication, however, was a big problem. Few locals spoke English and while Nick tried to pick up a few words of Russian, it proved a tough task. Even buying food was difficult – and the packs of duty-free cigarettes he'd brought over from Britain were no help. Everyone simply smoked dirt-cheap cigarettes from Afghanistan, so he ended up selling them to his workmates instead. But the main problem was that, in the food shops, everyone had to stand in interminable queues until they reached the front where the food would be on display behind the counter. You couldn't just pick up what you wanted; you had to ask for it. Even when Nick pointed to what he planned to buy, the shopkeepers often didn't seem to understand.

'The place was crazy fun, but the lack of communication made everything really, really hard work,' he says. 'I remember one evening coming home from work with Nolan and I was starving. So I said I'd go down to the local shop. At the counter, I saw what I thought was a big chunk of cheese so I pointed to that, eventually made myself understood, and they wrapped it up for me, and I paid. And when I got home, I was so excited about this cheese. But as soon as I bit into it, I discovered it was lard.'

Gradually, Nick picked up a smidgen more of the Russian language and started venturing further afield. He studied the maps of the Moscow Metro, the underground train system that ran throughout the city, and would catch trains to different stations to explore.

The one thing that shocked him more than anything else was the level of homelessness in Moscow. There were so many people sleeping on the streets, far more than he'd ever seen back in England or in Australia during his time there. He'd always had the idea that Russia's communist past would ensure there weren't huge gaps between rich and poor, but that certainly didn't look to be true. He often saw small groups of people huddled by station entrances, shivering in the wind, asking passers-by for money. It was hard to believe such poverty existed in a city that otherwise looked extremely wealthy.

Nick slowly began to learn more and more about the country and its inhabitants. Having lost his own children, something that was still never far from his mind, he was touched by the way Russians placed huge value on the importance of family, with all members closely involved in one another's lives. Children were absolutely doted on by their parents and grandparents, who considered bringing them up well as one of the most important roles in life. Often three generations would live together in one household, and the wellbeing and happiness of the children would be everyone's priority. Moreover, if any one of the extended family was ever in need, the rest would rally round to make sure they were properly looked after.

Nick couldn't help comparing that to his own wider family. His father, John Stride, had been serving as an RAF electronics engineer stationed in Singapore with his wife Judith when his second son Nick was born there on 25 March 1968. Two years later, they returned to Britain to settle in Devon and then moved to Southampton in 1977 when Nick was nine years old, his brother Andy was eleven and his sister Claire was eight. Nick was never close to anyone in his family and felt very much the black sheep, with his love of the atlas and his dreams of one day travelling the world. The others never seemed interested in anywhere further than their own city or the annual holiday on the same campsite in France every year. By contrast, Nick was an energetic, outgoing kid who loved fishing, hunting and anything to do with the Great Outdoors. He also adored photography and with a little camera he bought after saving up for months, he'd go to the motor races and take pictures of the cars. His father was dismissive of his hobby. 'You should forget that,' he'd tell the boy. 'You won't ever make any money out of taking photos.'

His dad wasn't a particularly loving man. He'd been scarred by his own father, James Stride, a soldier who'd fought at the horrific-ally bloody Battle of Monte Cassino in a series of military assaults against the Nazis in Italy. He'd even been featured in a newsreel shown back in England, picked out from the regiment as the biggest soldier there. Big Jim had also been captured twice, including in North Africa, and managed to escape on both occasions. But when the declared war hero finally returned home, he was a changed man, a heavy drinker given to violent rages against his wife Ena and to beating his three sons. Nick's dad, as the eldest, bore the brunt of that, and eventually ran away from home to join the forces and escape his father's wrath. He never forgave him. It was only towards the end of Nick's grandfather's life that they uncovered a secret.

In the run-up to Christmas, they saw their grandfather signing cards with the name Jim Gladwin Stride. 'We thought he must be going senile – now he can't even remember his name,' Nick says. 'But then my dad pulled him up on it, and he said, "Oh, we're not Strides." Dad asked, "What do you mean?" And he said, "I never told you, but when I was a baby, I was left in a shoebox outside The Red Lion Pub, below Bargate in Southampton, and I was adopted by the Stride family." We were all dumbfounded. But then he said when he was in his teens, he tried to track down his real family, and their name was Gladwin. So he must have had a pretty tough life, all in all.'

Equally, Nick's mum Judith was also carrying around a lot of baggage from her parents. When she was just six years old, her mother Frances, the daughter of wealthy Nottinghamshire land-owners the Heron family, abandoned her only child and chartered accountant husband Robert Buxton and ran off with one of the directors of the massive Whitbread Brewery company. Judith, like Nick's dad did with his father, forevermore held a grudge. Granny Law, as she was known to the family after her wedding to her new lover in 1954, became something of a celebrated personality in the UK. She climbed the six highest peaks in Europe, raced a motor-cycle in the Isle of Man TT races and appeared in the George Formby music comedy film *No Limit,* which made the legendary actor, singer and comedian a star.

After her husband died, however, she'd visit the family for two weeks every year from where she was living in Nottingham. Nick's parents allowed her to stay but never really had much time for her. They considered her eccentric and strange and didn't take much notice of her. Nick was quite the opposite.

'My parents despised her past and her personality, my father most of all,' he says. 'She'd come down when Wimbledon was on as she loved tennis but didn't have a TV. Unfortunately, my dad hated tennis, which didn't help. She was a strange character and lived almost as a recluse and didn't even have a record player, nor any clue about money and the cost of living. When she came, she used to sit and drink Dad's homemade beer, which he'd complain about but he'd never stop her. As soon as she'd arrive, everyone would dis-appear, but I never understood why. I found her fascinating. I'd sit there, holding her hand, listening to all her stories for hours. Even if half of them weren't true, they were incredible. I loved it.

'But nobody else had any time for her. I'd be thinking Nan was such an interesting lady, so different to anyone I'd ever met, while the rest of the family were saying she was crazy. Whenever Mum wanted to have a go at me – like the time, as a young kid, I put cement into the washing machine, copying Dad putting it in his cement mixer – she'd say I was just like my grandmother. Eventually, Dad cut granny's time with us from two weeks to one, and then, finally, wouldn't let her visit at all. When I was fourteen, she died and I refused to go to the funeral which infuriated my father. I said I'd always been there for her when she was alive as she was so amazing, and he was only going to her funeral out of guilt. For the next two years, he refused to speak to me, and he walked past me in the house every day without saying a word. But Granny Law left a legacy of over half a million pounds, mostly in shares, which my father kept a secret from me, until one day, I broke into my parents' security box and discovered them. Meanwhile, my mum passed me an envelope saying Granny had left a little money and my father was gifting us, his children, a thousand pounds each. I refused to take it. I felt it was Nan's money and it wasn't his to give.'

Russian families, in contrast, seemed a great deal more normal, loving and tight-knit. Sometimes, Nick found it almost painful to see Russian families out walking together, with grandparents, their children and grandchildren all talking and laughing at the same time. He wondered if, one day, he'd ever have a family life like that of his own.

At those times, he became quiet and morose and thought back to his own lost children, before making a determined effort to shake himself out of it and back into the present. As it was, he was on a contract for ten weeks on and two weeks off, but no one was ever paid for the two weeks when they weren't working. Nick wasn't keen on going back to the UK for a break anyway, as he had no desire at all to see his own family, so decided very soon after arriving in Russia that he'd simply work all the way through and earn as much as he could.

Every evening, however, when he came back to his quiet apartment after those expeditions to see Moscow, or a quiet drink in a bar, he tried to concentrate on what the future might hold. But finally, he realised he had to admit his most pressing problem: he was terribly, horribly lonely.

# THREE

## BACK IN THE USSR

**IT WASN'T LONG BEFORE** nearly all the men who'd come over to Russia with Nick – even the married ones – had girlfriends. The only two who didn't were Nick and his mate Nolan. They discussed it several times, and agreed they weren't interested. While many of the women were beautiful, conversation was usually extremely limited by the language barrier. In addition, the others told them local women looking for foreign boyfriends were often interested only in what their new men might buy them.

'But whatever the truth of that, I really wasn't interested in meeting a woman,' Nick says. 'To be honest, I wasn't looking for a relationship. That was the last thing on my mind. I felt so alone and lost, but I'd had enough of relationships. I found Russian women fascinating as they're so straightforward and absolutely honest and not into playing games. They say exactly what they feel. But I knew they weren't going to be for me.'

Nick was still wrapped up in working and, in his downtime, exploring Moscow. He visited the Kremlin fortress with its high red walls, the windswept Red Square and the four glorious cathedrals where the country's old tsars were married, crowned and buried. He was dazzled by the Palace Armoury, glittering with history's treasures. There were weapons, paintings, Ivan the Terrible's ivory throne and bear-fur-lined coat, Catherine the Great's carriages, embroidery studded with pearls, the magnificent silver gowns of the last of the ill-fated tsars, the Romanovs, and a collection of ten of the most exquisitely ornate, delicately carved, priceless Faberge eggs. So many riches, little wonder the peasants were revolting.

He smiled to himself at his joke but then winced. It wasn't really any laughing matter. He'd earlier read how the last tsar and his family met their fate: told to pose in their finery for a photograph but then shot with guns rather than cameras by their jailors, with the survivors bludgeoned to death.

The fabulous St Basil's Cathedral, a swirling candy cane of eye-popping colours and architectural flourishes, was always worth a visit, and he loved having a coffee in the square and gazing at the elaborate turrets that felt so familiar from his atlas at home. Another day, he admired the world's best collection of Russian art at the State Tretyakov Gallery and then rented a bicycle to race around Gorky Park. He was disappointed that he didn't recognise it better from the movie of the same name in which a Moscow militsiya officer, played by William Hurt, goes to the ice rink at the park to view three bodies. Later, he realised why nothing looked familiar: the film had been made in Helsinki and Stockholm, as the Soviet Communist Party had branded the plot 'anti-Russian' and banned the crew from the country.

Wherever he went, there seemed to be both light and dark. There were remnants of a gloriously wealthy past, side-by-side with stories of the misery of the impoverished proletariat. He was startled by such an incredible length and breadth of history, by the soaring highs and crashing lows. While around him he could see Muscovites in their furs and expensive suits being proud tourists in their own city, he was also constantly assailed by beggars asking for a few roubles to buy vodka or bread – usually in that order. All in all, Russia was a staggering place, he felt.

But back in 1998, it was also in a great deal of trouble. It had been only seven years since the Soviet Union had collapsed and its republics had seceded. President Mikhail Gorbachev had resigned, Boris Yeltsin was elected President of the newly named Russian Federation, while a highly ranked intelligence officer with the KGB called Vladimir Putin resigned the position he had held for sixteen years to enter politics.

Now, with Yeltsin in charge and Putin installed as the first deputy chief of the presidential staff, the country remained in an almost constant state of flux. The economy was in dire straits after the war in Chechnya cost it an estimated US$5.5 billion, while huge budget deficits, the 1997 Asian financial crisis, financial mismanagement and the falling prices of crude oil and non-ferrous metals had severely depleted the country's reserves of foreign exchange. On the streets, Nick could see the evidence everywhere, from the peasants drifting into the city to seek their fortune after a devastating drop in federal subsidies for agriculture, to the coal miners striking over unpaid wages and blockading the Trans-Siberian Railway, to the crowds of kids begging outside every McDonald's.

Even though Nick could still speak barely any Russian, he could feel the uneasiness around Moscow. People seemed desperate for money. One day, he came out of the Chancery and started helping the Russians working outside.

'Thank you,' one of them told him, slapping him on the back. 'You good man. I have a daughter. You want to meet her?'

Nick tried his best to look flattered. 'Thanks so much,' he replied. 'But no, not really.'

'But she is very nice,' the man insisted. 'You will like her. She is a nurse.'

'That's great, Nick replied. 'But I'm sorry, I don't have any free time.'

It happened constantly, and Nick turned down offers of nurses, office workers, students and even a mechanic. 'They were just desperate for money,' he says. 'They all wanted to get their daughters married off to a foreigner as they assumed you were rich – or richer than them, at least. People were pretty poor out there at the time, and always looking for a way to make a bit extra.

'But all in all, Russians are a strange bunch. When you talk to them, or somehow become their friend, they become the most loyal, generous friend you've ever met. They'll do anything for you. It's remarkable. But then if you don't know them, they'll do anything not to look at you, or speak to you, and can be your worst enemy. If you were lying injured on a road, they'd ignore you or walk over you. We were told there was a Russian law that says that if someone's injured, say in a car accident, and you touch them, then you can be liable for their death if something happens to them.'

One day, close to the British Embassy, Nick saw a worker fall off scaffolding on a building site. He rushed over to see if anything could be done but when he arrived, he could see the man was clearly on his last few breaths. 'I wanted to help, but everyone shouted at me to get away,' Nick says. 'There was nothing I could do. They told me I'd have to be gone by the time the police arrived because otherwise I'd be arrested, and probably have money extorted out of me. So, I left. There seemed no alternative.'

As the weeks passed, Nick learnt more and more words of the Russian language – he'd set himself the target of ten a day – and enjoyed being in a place that was so unfamiliar in every way. He missed company, however, with so many of his workmates out drinking or on the prowl for women every night. One evening, another English émigré from another company, Jim, insisted Nick and Nolan join him and his mates. He had a wife back in the UK, but also a long-term girlfriend in Moscow, Natasha, and seemed to have no moral difficulty with this arrangement. It was Natasha's birthday and a crowd were meeting at the jazz bar Fat Mo's. He assured Nick he'd have a good time and while Nick was dubious, he agreed to go.

He arrived just after everyone else and was surprised, upon entering, to see all the English men standing up at the bar, drinking, and Natasha with nine other Russian women sitting around a table, waiting for the men to join them.

Nick went over to Jim. 'Aren't you going to go and have a drink with your girlfriend?' he asked him.

'Nah, not yet,' Jim replied. 'I need another few drinks first.'

Nick looked over his shoulder and saw all the men were steadily becoming more and more inebriated. He saw Natasha looking anxious and went over to her to wish her a happy birthday. Immediately, his attention was caught by a stunningly beautiful woman sitting to her left. She was tall and slim with ash-brown hair to her shoulders. They locked eyes and he felt his heart skip a beat.

'Tasha,' he said when he could take a breath, 'could you introduce me to your friend?'

Natasha smiled. 'Of course,' she said. 'With pleasure.'

Nick spent the rest of the evening talking to – or at – Ludmila. 'It was so strange,' he says now. 'We both felt we had an instant connection, even though we couldn't really talk or understand what each other was saying. We spent all our time not so much *talking* as *gesturing*. Then we put a Russian-English dictionary between us, both trying to make ourselves understood. It was ridiculous but we both laughed and did our best to communicate. She was unlike anyone I'd ever met before. She was just so straight to the point, like a breath of fresh air, and so fearless.'

Tasha was keen for them to go off and spend the night together, but neither Nick nor Ludmila was interested. Somehow, they managed to make each other understand that neither wanted to get together unless they had a proper relationship. 'I had so much respect for Luda,' Nick says. 'She didn't care about money or what I might buy her; there was nothing like that. She was completely the opposite. She wanted to get to know me, and that felt so refreshing. We just seemed to hit it off straight away.'

From that evening on, Nick and Luda were almost inseparable. Apart from her smoking, which Nick hated, the hardest thing was arranging dates on the phone. Nick would suggest where and when they'd meet, using his English-to-Russian dictionary, and she'd respond, which he'd then have to try to decipher with his Russian-to-English version. As a result, Nick's Russian improved in leaps and bounds – out of necessity more than any linguistic flair – and gradually they were able to speak to each other and comprehend more and more.

Of course, Nick knew very little about her. He knew her mother had been ill, and she hadn't known her father, so the only real family she had was her grandmother, living in the small town of Tsimlyansk in south-western Russia. She was also open and honest to a fault. Yet at the back of his mind was always the worry that she could be a spy for the Russian Government, but then he knew she didn't have much money so, even if she was one, she'd be on a pretty lowly rank. But, as per the protocol, he took her passport in one day to the British Embassy for her to be checked out and felt enormously relieved when she was cleared.

'It took quite a while, though, for me to understand what she did for a job,' Nick says. 'I remember going to meet her one day from work and it was a huge building and on the front door it had a sign, something like Academy of Nuclear Science. I thought, *Oh my God, she's a scientist! How brilliant is that!* But then when I spoke to her about it, she said no. The Academy had run out of money, and they were renting out rooms to other companies. What she actually did was work as a censor for Russian television. She had to view and study programs, and there was a list of things she had to look out for and remove.'

It was much more fun looking around Moscow with a Russian, someone who could understand the signs on the Metro so they'd actually make it to the spots they were aiming for. The pair visited Victory Square spreading from the Triumphal Arch to the Victory Museum dotted with huge Soviet-style monuments, patriotic symbols and fountains. 'Back in the USSR', Nick hummed to himself as he took in the display of old Soviet military might. Then they explored the museum, with Europe's biggest collection of

World War II military equipment, including tanks, Soviet warplanes and captured enemy weaponry.

All the time, Luda pointed out some feature or other of the Metro system that Stalin built, one of the most efficient people-movers in the world. Travelling at speeds of up to eighty kilometres per hour, the trains crisscrossed the city for a length of nearly 400 kilometres on seventeen lines, with no fewer than forty-four of its 263 stations listed as cultural heritage sites.

Luda insisted on showing Nick the pick of those stations – Kievskaya, Novoslobodskaya, Komsomolskaya, Kurskaya and Revolution Square – with their great curving architecture, cavernous spaces, glowing pastel colours and chandeliers. Stalin had intended the stations to be underground 'people's palaces', and many certainly were, Nick had to admit. Even the journeys down to the platforms were an experience, with some of the stations going as deep as eighty-four metres underground, with dizzyingly long escalators carrying the crowds, and travelling at about twice the speed of the leisurely British or Australian equivalents.

But it was down on the platforms that the wonder really set in for Nick. Many of the stations were decorated with colourful mosaics of Soviet-era revolutionary images and heroes, extolling the virtues of work, family and community. Lenin bore down on commuters as they went about their business, while the power and the glory of the 1905 revolution – with strikes by workers, mutinies in the military and peasant uprisings – were celebrated with a fervour that seemed to Nick almost whimsical. Walls were inset with intricate tile work, creating beautiful patterns designed to lift the hearts of the lumpen proletariat, while elsewhere, there were stained-glass panels, not of religious iconography but of socialist symbols, portraits and scenes with ubiquitous red flags flapping in the background. In some stations there were lamps jutting from the walls, shaped like victory torches, and beautiful artworks that might elsewhere be reserved for galleries, displaying bloody – but heroic – scenes of military triumphs.

'The thing that always took me aback the most, however, were the carriages,' says Nick. 'There was something strange about them. Inside, they were almost bare, with absolutely no adverts on the walls. Maps of the system, yes, and treatises on the importance of further education, but no inducements to buy anything at all. Russia was endlessly fascinating. I honestly loved it. It felt like a very easy place to live. You just needed to know the rules and what would be dangerous and what wasn't.'

The work on the British Embassy was scheduled to take two years but by August 1998, six months into his contract, Nick started wondering if he could continue for much longer. While some things in Russia were improving – he and Luda even saw the Rolling Stones play at the Olympic Stadium after the band had been refused entry in 1967, and again in the 1970s – the Russian economy was in an absolute mess. Russia had been obliged to provide help to the former Soviet states by importing goods from them, financed by foreign loans. They were unable to pay back those loans, however, and, together with falling productivity, financial bungling and the high fixed exchange rate against foreign currencies, the Central Bank ended up devaluing the rouble on 17 August 1998, defaulting on its domestic debts and declaring a freeze on the repayment of foreign debt. Many banks went under as a result of the crisis, dubbed 'Russian flu', inflation soared to eighty-four per cent, Yeltsin came under renewed attack, and the country was forced to appeal for international aid, including for food.

'It was incredible,' Nick says. 'Roubles literally became worthless overnight, and there was a mad rush to try and get hold of US dollars. One of the Russian managers said he'd got news that there was one bank that still had US dollars, so we'd have to go now to get them. So, I went with him into the changing room and he got a pistol out of his cupboard. As he did so, four bullets fell on the floor. I picked them up and, as a joke, I said, "There's only four bullets here, what if there's five of them?" He didn't even smile. "No, no, you don't understand," he said. "We fire once, and they will all run away." We went to the bank and, thankfully, no one fired, and we did actually get about US$7000.

'But the worst thing was, there was no food; food just disappeared. Everyone went to the shops and bought it all. I remember sitting with the lads and pooling all our cash, and then sending people out to try to buy food. We thought we were going to starve to death. So we had emergency packages sent out to us at the embassy. But the day the first truck arrived, the crane picked up the big wooden crate of food on the back and then, inexplicably, dropped it down on the ground outside the embassy. Within seconds, the Russians were there, taking all the cans of food and the chocolates, everything. We could only sit and watch. There was nothing we could do. It would have been funny if we weren't so hungry.'

Luckily, the crisis died down quickly and everything – apart from the value of the rouble – slowly returned to normal. Nick and Luda lived on the Russian smoked braided cheese snack Chechil that a little kiosk next to his apartment sold, along with beer. But there were other strange things happening, too. Russian TV reported on the first anniversary of Princess Diana's death on

31 August, saying no one had remembered her, showing footage of empty London streets. Nick was appalled and mentioned it to his mum when she called. She was taken aback. 'No, it was the biggest celebration,' she told him. 'That avenue was lined with flowers.' It seemed the TV crew had filmed the streets in the early morning, weeks before. When he asked Luda, the TV censor, she quickly changed the subject.

There was trouble at work, too. The contracting company wouldn't provide any safety equipment and, with winter approaching and the prospect of temperatures that had in the past plunged in Moscow to as low as minus forty-two degrees, they were also refusing to buy cold-weather gear. Nick decided he'd had enough. It was time to move on.

But there was now one complication: Luda. And then he was arrested on charges of money laundering.

# FOUR
# A RIDDLE WRAPPED IN A MYSTERY

WHEN NICK HAD MADE his decision to leave Russia in November 1998, he sat down with Luda on the end of the bed in his apartment and held both her hands in his.

'Look, what are we going to do about our relationship?' he asked quietly in Russian, at which he'd, by now, become almost fluent. 'It's too hard for me to live here much longer, and if I go back to England, it's going to be even harder for you living with me there.'

He paused, then continued. 'All the visa regulations in different countries make it so difficult for us to be together, so we've got to make a choice. Tell me, what do you want to do?'

Luda looked back at him, evenly. There was a moment of silence. Then she squeezed his hands. 'I want us to stay together,' she whispered. 'I want to be with you.'

Nick's eyes filled with tears. That's exactly what he wanted, too. 'Okay, let's give it a go,' he said. 'How about we both leave work and travel for a bit together and see how it works out?' Luda nodded her head enthusiastically.

41

'I thought that would be a good test for us both,' Nick says now. 'If we survived that, and came back still very much in love, then I'd know we'd be pretty much committed to each other.'

Together they pored over a map and matched each country with the corresponding Russian visa regulations. It was just as he'd feared: for the more than thirty countries they looked at, there were only three or four Luda could visit without undergoing the gruelling visa-application process. As a result, they decided to spend three months touring Thailand, Malaysia and Indonesia – three countries for which Russian citizens didn't need a visa. Then Nick put in his resignation and flew to London to take some money out of his bank account back in the UK, where his pay was always deposited, since, at the time, there were no cash machines in Moscow to access it. On his return to Russia, he filled in the obligatory currency declaration form to say he was bringing £3000 into the country, then went straight to see Luda, bought two plane tickets and packed warm-weather gear.

They were both excited. Luda hadn't been overseas before, nor swum in an ocean, and was keen to get going. Nick was desperate to see the sun again, sit on warm sand and dive into the surf. The day they jumped into a taxi to travel the thirty kilometres outside Moscow to the Sheremetyevo Alexander S. Pushkin International Airport, their spirits were high.

But on arrival, things went rapidly downhill. Nick visited the empty men's toilets, went into a cubicle and then heard someone walk straight into the one next to his. The next moment, he saw a little mirror appear underneath the partition. It disappeared as quickly as it had appeared and, for a second, Nick thought he must have imagined it. And then it came back. Nick shouted and tried to kick it, and heard a scrabbling next door, the slamming of the door and a man's hurried footsteps towards the exit. Nick flung open his cubicle just in time to see the back of the man's head. He assumed he was from the internal police.

Nick started to feel uneasy and, as the couple went through customs and Nick handed in his currency form, the official gestured for the pair to stand aside.

'Is there a problem?' Nick asked the woman in Russian.

She scowled at him. 'Yes,' she said. 'This form is a fake.'

Nick was taken aback. 'No, it's not,' he countered. 'It's got your official stamp on it.'

'No, this form is a fake,' she repeated.

'No, it's not,' he insisted. At that point, he thought the officer might let them go. A regular tourist might by now have offered to pay a 'fine' to help them on their way, but it was obvious from Nick's Russian that he wasn't just visiting and was ready to argue the toss.

The three stood there, in silence. 'They don't talk,' Nick says. 'It's an approach designed to intimidate you. And, finally, security arrived and took us away, put us in a room and left us there. We stayed there for something like eight long hours. That's to scare you, too, and it's a really effective tactic. Then we were finally taken to another security guard who took down all our details on his computer – we could see him overriding all the details they already had – until he went away and left us for another four hours. Eventually, he returned and said we had two choices: either I could hand over the £3000 he knew I had on me, or I'd face a Russian court on charges of money laundering in three days' time. By then, I'd had enough. I told him to take my money.

'As I handed it over, I told him that, legally I was allowed to take out at least £500. He agreed, and said I could have that back. And then I said, "And the same for my partner?" He looked at Luda and nodded and gave me 1000. Then, bizarrely, he shook my hand and said, "Thank you for helping the Russian economy."'

Nick looked back at him, stunned, but he wasn't finished. 'What do you want to do now?' the official asked Nick.

'I want to get out of this country and go to Thailand, like we intended,' Nick replied. 'But thanks to you, we've missed our plane.'

'Do not worry,' said the man. 'I will help.' He then marched them over to the counter run by the Russian national carrier Aeroflot and demanded they reissue two tickets to Bangkok for the next day. But even that wasn't the end of their ordeal. He told them to sit and wait while he vanished with their passports. He didn't reappear for another fourteen hours, turning their detention into a total of twenty-six hours.

Once they were safely on the plane, Nick allowed himself to relax. He was angry but he'd half-expected what had unfolded. Frequently on the streets with Luda, he was stopped by police and 'fined' for not having the 'right' papers or his passport with him. Often, they'd demand 5000 roubles but then agree to be bartered down to 500 or sometimes just 100. He'd also been detained on what he felt were spurious grounds three times before.

'But this time, I was the most annoyed at myself,' he says. 'I should never have declared that money in the first place. I should have been more clued-up than that. They were just waiting for me to leave the country to get hold of it. It can be such a corrupt country.'

Thailand was a complete revelation for Luda. She'd only ever swum in the Don River in Tsimlyanskoy where she'd stayed with her grandmother, and she found she loved the ocean. That is, until she swam out further, could no longer see the bottom and panicked. It took a while for her to get used to being out of her depth. For Nick, it was a joy being back on a beach in the sunshine and enjoying easy-going coastal life. It reminded him, with a pang, of his time in Australia and his dream of going back there to live one day. One day. But in the meantime, the pair both enjoyed the relaxed, carefree spirit of the country, although it was never easy travelling on two such different passports.

After a month in Thailand, they caught a bus bound for Malaysia, but the bus was boarded by customs officials who asked all passengers to hold up their passports for examination. Luda was singled out because of her Russian passport and taken off the bus with her luggage. Nick picked up his bag and went with her. 'It was crazy,' he says. 'They said her passport must be fake because it wasn't in Russian. I told them it was a passport, an international document, so they were always in English. But while we were standing there, arguing, the bloody bus took off without us. I couldn't believe it. The officials eventually let us go, but then we had to hitchhike into Malaysia. Luckily, we got a lift on the back of a coconut truck.'

That wasn't the end of their difficulties, however. Their flight from Kuala Lumpur to Indonesia involved a stopover in Singapore. Russian passport-holders required a visa to get in, and Luda didn't have one. Customs officials in Singapore, as a result, detained her and took away her passport. Nick again protested on her behalf – he, after all, had been born in Singapore when his father was stationed there – and eventually she was allowed to stay for just thirty-six hours before heading off to Bali.

'We had an amazing time, staying in little cheap hostels, eating local food and enjoying the beaches,' Nick says. 'But travelling was stressful. It was always at the back of our minds that we'd have to go back the same way too. And, sure enough, on the way back via Singapore, she was detained again. This time, I'd told her if they did that, to just burst into tears and not stop crying. So she did, and they absolutely panicked and let her in.

'All in all, we had a brilliant time together and the relationship more than survived, it flourished. I loved every second we were spending together, and I felt we were just perfect for each other.'

On their way back to Bangkok, on one of the Phi Phi Islands, off the coast of Krabi in southern Thailand, they had dinner in a tiny restaurant late one evening, and Nick proposed. Luda accepted enthusiastically. But then Nick raised the one subject he'd been avoiding.

'I'd love to have a family with you, Luda,' he said.

'And yes, I would like that, too,' she replied. 'We will stand together forever.'

'But there's one problem. I'd have to ask you to stop smoking. I couldn't have children with someone who smokes.'

'Then I will stop, Nick.'

'Really? You'd do that?' Nick asked.

'Yes, I will just have one more,' she said, reaching for the packet.

Nick put his hand over hers. 'No, if you're serious about staying together and having children, don't take the last one.'

Luda looked steadily into Nick's eyes, then picked up the cigarette and threw it away. And that was the last evening she ever smoked.

The big problem, however, was where the couple would live. Nick didn't much fancy returning to Russia, but he knew it could take

46

a long time to get permission for Luda to join him in the UK. So, after talking it through, they agreed: Nick would return to the UK, sell everything he owned, settle all his affairs, and earn as much money as he could, while Luda went to stay at her grandmother's. Then Nick would come back to Russia and together they'd start the long process of applying for a UK visa. At the end of the holiday, it was a tearful farewell.

The pair were apart for three months as Nick raised as much money as he could. He worked for another glass company and saved every spare penny, cashed in his endowment policy and took all his savings out of the bank. At the same time, he had another stroke of luck. A house he'd paid a deposit on before going to Russia had been sold by the building society that was going to give him a mortgage, and they wrote saying they had a cheque for him for £6000.

'Then at the same time, I received a letter that my divorce had come through,' Nick says. 'It felt like everything was coming together. And it meant I could get back to Russia sooner, rather than later.'

Nick started making plans to fly to Moscow and phoned Luda to set the date for their reunion, but she said she had no money for the flight to the capital. He suggested she borrow some until he arrived, at which point he could repay her benefactor. But no one else where she lived had any money either. Nick was loath to post money out. The first time he'd been there, when the rouble had crashed and food was scarce, his mother had sent him little care packages which, when opened, were invariably full of birdseed, with a couple of magazines at the bottom. When he'd asked her on the phone why she was sending him such packages, she said she wasn't; she'd been posting food, chocolate, tea bags and magazines.

It appeared that the packages were being opened, rifled through, and all the goodies replaced with birdseed so the weight would be the same. Only the magazines, which the interceptors couldn't have read anyway, survived. Now, if Nick posted out money to Luda, he was sure it would be stolen, but there was no alternative. In the end, he sent her a little package of cheap tea bags, with US$200 hidden in the bottom, and happily the cash reached her intact.

After they met back up in Moscow in March 1999, the couple immediately started the process of applying for her UK visa through the British Embassy, the same building Nick had originally come to Russia to work on. To help prove they had a genuine relationship, Nick had kept all the phone cards he'd used calling Luda from the UK and emptied the huge bag over the examining official's desk. They also had photographs and souvenirs from their time both in Asia and Russia. No letters, though. Nick's Russian just wasn't up to that.

While they waited for the visa to come through, they rented a flat in Zelenograd, the largest, most populous suburb of Moscow, a two-hour bus ride from the centre. It was a dreary place dominated by tall apartment towers – Nick and Luda lived on the twenty-third floor of thirty – and was among the cheapest places in the city to live. But it was also crime-ridden and, at the time, had the highest murder rate of foreigners in the world. Nick would sleep with a carving knife placed within easy reach just under the bed, another on Luda's side, and two more hidden by the front door. On the streets outside, he'd be sure always to dress in a big black overcoat and a hat pulled down low over his forehead to try to look as Russian as he could, and never spoke for fear of being overheard and targeted.

Not everyone was fooled, however. One day, Nick was passing through Red Square with Luda when he spotted the maverick ultra-right-wing politician Vladimir Zhirinovsky – famous for throwing a glass of orange juice at an opposing politician in the Duma on TV – preaching the virtues of communism to a forty-strong crowd. He caught sight of Nick and yelled, 'Look! Look at the foreign bour-geoisie!' Everyone turned to stare. Nick was aghast.

'But how did he know I wasn't Russian?' he asked Luda later. 'I hadn't said anything, and all my clothes were Russian.'

She looked at him. 'Because,' she said flatly, 'you just don't look Russian.'

The visa process dragged on and on with little end in sight. Nick was brought into the embassy and asked a series of ques-tions about what Russian books Luda liked to read. He didn't have a clue. All his letters to his brother were examined minutely for any hint that his relationship wasn't genuine, and they even called Andy up to quiz him. One afternoon when Nick was in the office, he was approached by a man asking him if he'd like to buy a British Virgin Islands passport. He had no idea whether it was a genuine offer or a trick by officials to catch him out. He refused, curtly. No one could tell him, however, how long that elusive visa would take.

While he was waiting, Nick applied to the British consulate for permission to marry. As soon as that came through, he and Luda went to a featureless building in the city for their wedding on 6 June 1999. It was an unspectacular affair. They waited with other couples in a gloomy hall until their names were called out over the public address system and they were ushered into a room. There, they filled out a form, countersigned by an equally gloomy woman, and then they were sent back out. Nick sat back down in the hall until Luda asked him what he was waiting for.

'The ceremony,' he said. 'I hope it's not too long away.'

Luda burst into peals of laughter. 'No, that was it,' she explained. 'We are married now.'

Nick was perplexed. 'It's a bit of a comedown from weddings I've known,' he complained. 'She didn't even say I could kiss the bride.'

There wasn't much else to laugh about at the time. Life in Zelenograd was hard. Moscow was still in a state of financial crisis, with Vladimir Putin taking over as Prime Minister in August 1999, and the first people to suffer, Nick soon discovered, were those outside the centre. The heating for all the apartments in the city was via central power stations that pumped hot water into the buildings, through radiators and taps. But with all of them focused on the city centre, the couple hadn't had any hot water or heating for months. They'd sleep under piles of blankets and boil water on the stove to heat the water for a bath. Overnight, it was so cold that all water in the apartment, including any left in the kettle, would freeze.

The city was also in the grip of shock and fear from a series of explosions that went off in four apartment blocks in Moscow and two other major cities in September 1999, killing more than 300 people and injuring 1000 more. Another bomb was detonated in the amusement arcade of a major Moscow shopping centre, injuring thirty people, including several children, just two hours after Nick and Luda had been shopping there. An official investigation found the blasts were the responsibility of Chechen insurgents; others believed they were the work of supporters of Putin to justify a new war in Chechnya and boost his own popularity as a perceived hard man against the ailing President Yeltsin.

After that, Nick and Luda were a great deal more cautious when going into town, but it was hard to keep away from the crowds. The Metro was always jampacked, and sometimes it would take an hour to force their way from the escalator to the platform to catch a train. One particularly crowded day, Nick was struck by an idea. He shouted out, in Russian, 'Let us through! My wife is pregnant!' It worked a treat; the police pushed the rest of the crowd aside to let them go into a carriage especially reserved for frailer, or sick, passengers.

But when they were comfortably seated, Luda turned to her husband, her eyes wide.

'Nick!' she said. 'How did you know?'

# FIVE
# LOOKING FOR A HOME

**NICK AND LUDA FINALLY** boarded a plane on Christmas Eve 1999, bound for Britain. It had taken months of waiting, and a memorable meltdown from Nick at the British Embassy when he banged his fist on the desk and demanded Luda had the right to a visa as the spouse of a UK citizen, to make it finally happen. But when it did, they both had to be careful. By then, Luda was eight-and-a-half months pregnant – reason enough to deny her a visa and ban her from joining the flight – but she hid the bump in a big woolly jumper and baggy jeans.

'We were desperate by then to get away,' Nick says. 'We were panicking. I knew if she gave birth in Moscow that would mean the child would be Russian and that would be a whole new ballgame. We hadn't been able to tell anyone she was expecting. I'd also read that a very high proportion of births in Russia had complications and husbands weren't allowed anywhere near their wives when they had medical exams or actually gave birth, so it was a very different system.

'When we arrived in Britain, we went to visit my mum and dad and finally broke the news that Luda was having a baby. Mum was thrilled and started making all these plans, but I had to stop her and say that she didn't have time for that; the baby was due in two weeks. But the British medical system was fantastic. The doctors were horrified that Luda hadn't had any blood tests or scans, so they arranged all that immediately. Then we went to visit my grandad, Big Jim, to introduce him to Luda. He gave a big speech about how it was time to forgive and forget. I wondered what I'd done. But then he said that the Russians had done some terrible things during the Second World War, but Luda and I had his blessing.'

Michael was born on 6 February 2000 at Southampton Hospital. It was an easy birth, which was lucky since Luda still spoke little English and had no idea what the nurses were saying when they told her to push. Nick had to be there throughout to translate for both parties.

They then had to find a place to live and furnish it from scratch. Nick found a job with another glazing company and worked all the hours he could to get them set up. It left Luda alone with Michael most of the time and she was homesick for Russia. From there, all the news was that Putin had just become acting President on Yeltsin's resignation and then, less than four months later, he was elected in his own right to the position of President. England to Luda, however, felt a world away and, unable to converse with anyone, she became terribly lonely. The weather didn't help either: it rained non-stop for three weeks.

'Luda really struggled,' Nick says. 'She didn't like England at all. I think she hated every second of it. The hardest thing was communication. You take for granted being able to speak the language of the place you're in, but not being able to make yourself understood can be so frustrating. There were no other Russians living near us, and she found English women so different to Russians. They couldn't be less alike.'

Luda found everything about the culture mystifying. One morning, the little family walked with Michael in his buggy down a path together close to the river and every time they passed someone, Nick would say, 'Good morning', and they'd respond in kind.

That afternoon, Luda asked, 'How do you know so many people?'

Nick didn't understand. 'I don't know any of them,' he said.

'You must do,' she argued. 'You said good morning to them all.'

By contrast, Luda wouldn't dream of speaking to, or even being friendly towards, anyone she didn't know.

Then Luda fell pregnant again. It was so soon after Michael, even the doctor could hardly believe it. The couple was delighted. There was one fly in the ointment: when Luda had entered the country, she was given a permit for a year, and at the end of that year, had to apply for permanent residency. For that, she just had to prove she was still with her husband and provide a gas or electricity bill to verify her address. But with their gas and electricity both on a meter, they didn't have bills and, despite providing plenty of other evidence to confirm where they were living, British immigration ruled that she hadn't proved it to their satisfaction in time, and she had overstayed her visa and must reapply for a new visa from Moscow.

'It was sickening,' Nick says. 'We'd given them all this information, including medical cards and other bills, but they said it wasn't enough. It wasn't even enough that I'd received their refusal posted to our address! By then Luda was seven months pregnant and really shouldn't be flying anywhere. But she was suddenly unlawful in England.'

Their daughter, Anya, was born on 2 January 2001. It was a quick birth, even easier than Michael's, and both parents were thrilled. But having to look after two small children at home served only to heighten Luda's sense of isolation, while being unlawful meant she wasn't allowed to apply for Child Benefit. Nick was still working long hours too, and although she was trying to learn English, she wasn't making much progress. So, when Nick was headhunted by one of the managers he'd worked with on the embassy in Moscow, about another job in Russia, Luda was overjoyed at the prospect of returning to her homeland. Nick wasn't so keen but, again, it was excellent money on offer, and it would mean working again with his old mate Nolan, while solving all of Luda's problems.

'I thought this was a fantastic opportunity,' Nick says. 'Not only were we going back to Moscow, which would suit Luda so much better and it would be great for the kids having a mum who'd be so much happier, but I'd get to do a huge project for a really important person in the government. I saw it as a great move for us all.'

The children were excited at the thought of living somewhere new and because they'd grown up speaking Russian at home, and English outside, Nick felt they'd be well equipped for the change. They weren't seeing their grandparents so much by then, either, as Nick's mum and dad had moved to Cornwall, so they just talked occasionally on the phone.

The job was building a private house for a leading Russian politician called Igor Shuvalov, just outside Moscow. A wealthy lawyer and private entrepreneur, he'd previously served as a minister of the Russian Federation as chief of staff of the Government, and assistant to the President. By this time, his star was firmly on the rise with Putin, as deputy head of the presidential administration and the President's representative to the National Banking Council. He was having a huge house built in the middle of sweeping gardens, complete with an Olympic-sized swimming pool, and winter gardens fashioned in marble and glass and topped with a vast glass dome that contained six different climatic zones. It would be Nick's task, as the specialist construction glazier, to coordinate all the work for the winter gardens and liaise with the Russian builders and the suppliers of materials in Europe.

It took two years to prepare for the project, with several trips to Belgium to oversee design and constant contact with Moscow. Nick and Luda kept an eye on everything happening in Russia and were, like most other people, shocked to hear of the assassination of the politician Sergei Yushenkov close to his house in the city in April 2003. He'd been investigating the apartment-block bombings the couple had lived through and had claimed they were the work of the FSB. He alleged operatives had planted the bombs to increase support for Putin's Second Chechen War, and Putin himself. He was killed by a single shot to the chest. Just over a year later, in July 2004, they were horrified again to hear of another assassination, this time of Paul Klebnikov, the chief editor of the Russian edition of *Forbes* magazine. He'd been writing about corruption in Russia and the lives of wealthy Russians. The Committee to Protect Journalists concluded he'd died in a contract killing.

During this time, Nick went on two forays to Russia to check on the site and its progress. On the first trip to Moscow, Nick was told he'd have to meet Shuvalov to win his approval. He waited at the office at the appointed time . . . and waited . . . and waited. Shuvalov finally turned up at 10pm, five hours late. He swept past Nick as one of the site managers said, 'Ah, this is Nick . . .' to his departing back. That, it turned out, was the much-awaited meeting. A few months later, Shuvalov travelled to London as President Putin's personal representative to the G8 summit, also attended by US President George W. Bush and UK Prime Minister Tony Blair.

Eventually it was decided that Nick, Luda, Michael, by now nearly six years old, and Anya, almost five, would move to Moscow in December 2005. They settled into an upmarket apartment building not far from the city centre, within easy commuting distance to the work site. The project was an enormous undertaking. Nick had previously worked on big developments, such as new wings for the Leeds General Infirmary, but this was in another league.

Conditions for the 200-odd workers were quite startling, too. No one was ever allowed to utter Shuvalov's name; they had to refer to him as 'The Client'. They were never to take any photos and had to be where they were supposed to be at any given time. Anyone wandering outside their prescribed area would have security personnel appearing magically within seconds to escort them back to where they should be. Such strict control over everyone's movements was a source of endless fascination for Nick. It wasn't like Nick could blend in easily, either; he turned out to be the only European there. Those in charge were from Russia, while the rest were cheap labour from the republics of Dagestan, on the Caspian Sea by Georgia, or Azerbaijan nearby.

But Nick soon realised why he was in so much demand. The Russians operated a strict hierarchy where the only person allowed to speak to a manager would be the person directly below him. Nick, as the sole European, was able to bypass that rule. He had numerous conversations with Shuvalov but was startled, one evening, to see his boss on TV, speaking perfect English. Up until then, Nick had assumed Shuvalov didn't know any of the language as the two had conversed only in Russian. 'That was a huge surprise,' Nick says now. 'But thinking about it, it was like an inferiority thing. He wouldn't deign to speak English to me because there's a good chance I'd be better at it than him. And that wouldn't do at all.'

On the greater Russian stage, there were further troubling events that Nick couldn't help being disturbed by. In October 2006, another Russian journalist who'd been critical of Putin was murdered. Anna Politkovskaya had accused him of turning Russia into a police state. The judge at the trial of the five men convicted of her murder found it was a contract killing but said it was a mystery who'd paid the US$150,000 fee.

A month later, there was yet another death, this time of the British-naturalised Russian defector Alexander Litvinenko, a former FSB agent granted asylum in the UK. Like Yushenkov, Litvinenko had accused the Russian secret services of staging the apartment bombings to elevate Putin. He also alleged that Putin had ordered the assassination of Politkovskaya. He died three weeks after drinking a cup of tea at a hotel in London that had been laced with the deadly poison polonium-210. Later, a British inquiry determined he'd been poisoned by two FSB agents on orders 'probably approved by . . . President Putin'.

It was alarming stuff, but Nick was surprised that his Russian workmates and friends seemed largely untroubled by it. 'I think

Russians are the least curious people in the world,' he says now. 'Honestly, it's incredible. Sometimes, I wanted to ask them, "Don't you find it strange that I'm a European doing this job in Russia?" But they just didn't want to know anything about it. I think it goes back to the Soviet communist days when you had to toe the line and wouldn't say anything to anyone. As a result, you just don't even ask.

'But for me, it was a great job,' Nick says. 'Technically, we were installing glass in a way that had never been done in Russia before, so the standard was challenging and absolutely exceptional, and being a part of that was really good. And as the expert in this, I was in charge. Interestingly, too, the Russians didn't see me as being European. They saw me as Russian almost immediately. I think I fitted the mould. I could speak Russian well by now, I was married to a Russian woman and I was different to most of the Europeans they'd met travelling the world. But most of all, I think it was the fact that now they could see I wanted to be there and to live in Moscow and I was happy to be there.'

Luda was also much more content, and the pair started thinking about schools for Michael and Anya. Most foreigners sent their children to European or American schools, but they both wanted theirs to go to Russian state schools and learn Russian and get to know other Russian kids. The schools, however, turned them down, saying they should go to European ones. Outraged, Luda wrote to the Minister of Education, whose office wrote back saying they should be allowed to attend a public school. That letter did the trick.

Michael fitted straight in at his new school. His Russian was good as Nick had supervised English lessons at home in the evenings to make sure his son kept up that language, too, and he made friends quickly. Sometimes, these friendships could be a worry, though. One day, when Nick was walking Michael home from school, the boy said his friend Roma's dad had a gun – and could he go around to his house to play with it? Nick's reaction was instant: No! But Michael was unperturbed.

'Roma's going to join the Russian army when he grows up,' Michael said. 'And I'm going to join the British army. And then we're all going to get together and bomb Dagestan.'

Nick was alarmed, stopped walking and bent down to talk to his son on the same level. 'Who do you think lives in Dagestan?' Nick asked him.

'I don't know,' Michael said.

'I do,' Nick replied. 'It's people like your sister, people like your mother, and families like ours.'

He could see Michael was thinking about that and the next day, when Nick met him, Michael said he'd changed his mind about what he wanted to do when he grew up.

'I've told Roma that when we leave school, we'll both become firemen and help people,' he declared.

'That's an excellent idea,' Nick said.

Anya found school more difficult as her Russian wasn't quite as good as her brother's, and she struggled a little more academically as a result, but she still seemed perfectly happy. She'd often come home with little notes written in Russian on scraps of paper, saying, 'I love you. I want to marry you.'

'We'd ask her where she got these from and who gave them to her,' Nick says. 'And she'd say some boy or other. She was a pretty little girl, and the only English girl in the school, which made her the centre of attention for a lot of the kids. They all seemed to love her.'

The family embarked on regular outings around Moscow to explore their new home, and sometimes got together with the families of Luda's friends or Nick's workmates. Even the biting Moscow winter now seemed bearable.

Michael remembers loving the snow. 'It was so much fun, playing snowballs and doing snow angels,' he says. 'We'd go to Victory Park where there was a huge hill and they'd put waterholes in the top to create ice slides. In the playground, they'd pour water over the slide too so we could all race down. As a kid, it really was a great time. Because the temperature is so extreme, you put on five layers of clothing and you're able to play outside and the snow's really dry, not sleety like it had been in England.'

School was strict but Michael enjoyed it, mostly. 'There were a lot of fights between kids, usually the Russians against those from Turkmenistan and Tajikistan who were mostly Muslims, but I was pretty lucky as both sides seemed to love me. I think they thought it was cool that I was an English kid. So I made friends of all races, and they left me out of the fights.'

Anya too found her Englishness an advantage. 'The other kids had never seen an English person before, so I was very interesting to them and they all wanted to befriend me and they stuck up for me. Some of the teachers were very grouchy, screaming at the class until we were all quiet. But I loved the snow in Moscow. Looking back, I think it was the best time of my life. Yes, it was cold in winter, but the snow made it magical, with all those big, fancy, elegant buildings, and it was always warm in the apartment.'

With the children adapting well to their new lives, Luda bliss-fully happy to be back in Russia and Nick enjoying his new job, he regularly pinched himself to think how well everything had turned out. For at that time, there was absolutely no inkling at all of the storm clouds gathering on the horizon.

# SIX

# MOTHER RUSSIA, FATHER PUTIN

BY THE START OF 2008, two years on from Nick and his family's arrival in Russia, everything was still looking rosy. Putin was approaching the end of his second four-year term as President – with eight years the constitutional maximum – and the economy had begun to surge. He'd enacted a number of far-reaching reforms, the price of Russian-produced oil and gas had increased fivefold, and he'd led a war that had unleashed a tidal wave of patriotic fervour against Chechen separatists.

On the ground, Nick admired the man's resolve. He'd always been disturbed by the number of beggars on the streets and the hungry children waiting outside McDonald's for any kindly patrons to pass them some scraps. It seemed Putin didn't like that either and vowed publicly that this would end. And almost overnight, it did. The beggars vanished, and Nick assumed they'd been given somewhere to live, hot meals and social security benefits. He could see standards of living steadily rising and the oligarchs being sidelined. Like the rest of the Moscow population, Nick joined the chorus of praise for Putin, whose apparent wisdom and benevolence were changing Russia for the better.

Michael, approaching his eighth birthday, and Anya, just turned seven, were relieved too. Walking to and from school every day, they'd had to weave their way past all the people living on the streets. 'I found it quite scary sometimes,' Anya says today. 'They were always after alcohol or drugs, and they could get quite aggressive. But I was always glad to have a Russian mum as she was pretty feisty and very protective of us, and it was great when there was less of them.'

At work, besides all the glass construction, Nick was being entrusted with increasingly high-level financial tasks for Shuvalov. Staff would come to him if they saw a problem, like an invoice being erroneously paid twice, and ask him to sort it out. As a result, he was party to a huge amount of personal information, and even access to his boss's bank accounts. 'It was all good at first, but then I think The Client's people started thinking that I might leave one day, and they worried about how much I knew,' Nick says. 'I could see them starting to get a bit paranoid around me, and I thought, *This isn't good . . .*'

When they had to go for meetings overseas, they started taking Nick with them. He was startled by the behaviour of some of them: ordering a restaurant's most expensive champagne and far more food than they could ever eat; walking into a jewellery store and asking for the biggest-ticket watch; and generally indulging in the kind of excess that never failed to attract attention. He'd try to coach them on European customs and standards, but they rarely listened.

Meanwhile, back in Russia, his special position at the company – outside of the hierarchy – wasn't making him popular with his workmates. He was generally viewed as being under Shuvalov's umbrella of protection, so a lot of the workers didn't want to talk to him any longer, suspecting he might report their conversations. For Nick, work life was becoming lonelier.

Then, in May 2008, the stakes suddenly skyrocketed. Because Putin wasn't allowed to be president for another term, he became Prime Minister and appointed Shuvalov as his deputy, while Dmitry Medvedev came in as President. All the talk at the work site was about how Shuvalov was being groomed by Putin to be not only his second-in-command, but also his eventual successor. After that, Shuvalov became even more remote. If the six-metre-high double doors that led onto the site weren't opened at exactly the moment his car pulled up, he often drove right on by and, whenever he did come on site, all the workers, except his most trusted aides, his security detail and Nick, had to leave. Sometimes it seemed he'd come only to have a wander around and walk his dogs, always followed closely by his security heavies. One day, Nick wasn't paying attention and slipped in between him and one of his minders. Immediately, the bodyguard opened his jacket to reveal his pistol in a chest holster. Another day inspectors came in to tick off some of the building work, and Nick was told not to speak to anyone.

'Everything was so absolutely secret,' Nick says, 'so it was no wonder that paranoia was starting to creep in. There was a bit of jealousy, too, as the other workers could see this European from nowhere being given preferential treatment and doing well. On site, one of the Russian managers kept coming on and pulling everything I'd done apart. I told the bosses that if he came and tried that again, I'd walk. It didn't really make me any more popular.

But there's still this deep-seated suspicion about Europeans; I think it's an historical thing. Taxi drivers would sometimes have a go at me, saying I wasn't Russian and should go back home. In the supermarket queue once, I had sixteen items in my basket rather than fourteen, and the worker there asked Luda who I was and demanded that she order me to go back home. Luda gave her short shrift.'

Strange things began to happen. One morning, on Nick's regular ride to work on the number 205 bus, Shuvalov's head of security got on and sat down next to him. The man usually arrived at the site in a chauffeur-driven limousine, so Nick was immediately on his guard. At the last stop, both men alighted the bus and started to walk the 800 metres to work.

'Tell me, Nick,' the man said, 'do you miss England?'

'No, not really,' Nick replied.

'But you must miss rugby.'

'I suppose so,' Nick agreed.

'And you must miss playing at number 12.'

Nick was stunned. How on earth would this man know the position he always played? 'Later on, I realised that they must have researched everything they could in my background,' Nick says now. 'I think that was intended to be a little bit of intimidation. Just to let me know, in the least subtle way possible, that they'd done some serious checking-up on me.'

With Nick spending such long hours at the site and doing his best to keep his head down while he was there, Luda decided she couldn't sit around in the apartment every day waiting for the kids to come home from school, or her husband to finish work. The couple set up a website, Moscow Fashion, and Luda would collect children's clothes and toys from all around the city to resell from home. When the children were around, they often accompanied her on these expeditions.

'We never had a vehicle, so we'd travel everywhere on the Metro or the bus from one side of the city to the other,' Michael says. 'We'd visit warehouses and stores and all sorts of places. It was a real experience. But the one thing I always hated about Moscow was the packs of stray dogs roaming the streets, and some would even ride the Metro too. There were so many dogs, according to some estimates about 35,000, and they were everywhere. Some of the old babushkas [grandmothers] fed the dogs so they'd become protective of certain people in the neighbourhood. A lot of the dogs were very aggressive, and they'd be snarling as you walked past them. One of them even bit Dad on his leg one day. Luckily, it didn't have rabies, but that was a bit of a scare. I was terrified. I imagine a lot of the Russian kids were frightened too, but they didn't roam as far as we did so probably didn't see them so much.'

The family also went out together regularly, visiting the Kremlin, and all the great tourist sights around Moscow. One day, they were out walking when they passed an old rundown building. Nick peered inside and saw what he thought looked like a horror show – a horde of people dressed in rags, many of them with obvious disabilities, jammed in and sleeping on the floors. He realised, with a start, that these were probably the beggars he'd so fondly imagined were now revelling in a better life. They'd simply been rounded up and dumped somewhere else.

At that point, Nick started talking about Australia, and saying sometime in the future he'd like to take them all for a holiday or even to live there. He told the children about the beaches, the kangaroos, the koalas and the outback. 'It's an amazing country,' he told them, wistfully. 'We'll see it together one day.'

Occasionally, in his time off, Nick was dragged into a few of the friendly rugby matches that were played around Moscow, although he never played at number 12 again. At one of these games, he met a young Georgian student called Giorgi, who was keen to learn about business from a European and zeroed in on Nick.

Today, Giorgi remembers Nick fondly. 'I liked him a lot,' he says. 'He was very friendly and funny and laughed and joked a lot, which is very different to the Russians, who can be very grumpy. We both loved rugby, and we formed a strong friendship through that. A couple of months later, he offered me a job – as a student in my last year of university, I always needed more money – and so we started to work together too. He was a good boss, demanding but also a very nice person with a lovely family.'

One day, Giorgi mentioned plans for a new construction project that was causing a great deal of excitement over in Georgia, and the fact that it needed some skilled tradespeople to help make it happen. It was a scheme the Georgian President, US-educated Mikheil Saakashvili, was extremely enthusiastic about. He'd come to power after leading the 2003 'Rose Revolution' and had embraced all things Western – particularly investment. And Giorgi, who turned out to be extremely well connected, said that Saakashvili was keen to meet Nick.

The Georgian leader had an ambitious plan to transform what had long been a dark, dingy and impoverished corner of the former Soviet Union into a brave new world of flashy casinos on the country's picturesque Black Sea coast, just over the border from Turkey. With Turkey dominated by Muslims, and thus a country where gambling was forbidden, Saakashvili imagined building a casino on the seafront at Batumi that would bring visitors flooding in and provide a rich source of new wealth. Nick, already working for, and obviously trusted by, such a high-profile Russian politician as Shuvalov, could be just the man Saakashvili needed to supervise that project, and then many more government initiatives to follow in his ambitious scheme to modernise the country.

'It sounded like a very big deal,' Nick says. 'It would be a huge job, and one that could go on for many years. It could be a neat solution to moving on from Russia, too. Things were just feeling too precarious there. People seemed to be so suspicious of me, and their paranoia felt as if it was mounting all the time, and there was nothing I could do to dampen it down. I worried about Luda and the kids. It suddenly didn't feel safe anymore. It was time to get out.'

A major difficulty, however, was how to get from Russia to Georgia to be interviewed by the President's people. Since the start of August that year, war had broken out between the two countries in the northern part of the republic. Fighting had continued until 16 August when a peace plan, brokered by France, was finally signed by the two sides, although Putin had effectively annexed two areas of Georgia, South Ossetia and Abkhazia in the north. Hostilities were as fierce as they'd ever been.

The borders between the two countries were still closed, so Nick realised the only solution was to fly to Armenia, the country to Georgia's south, and then catch another flight north to the Georgian capital Tbilisi. Giorgi had planned to accompany him, but he'd been suddenly called back home to fight. 'The war started so I had to leave the country,' says Giorgi. 'But I thought this job would be good for Nick. It involved a lot of glazing, which was his speciality.'

Arrangements were made instead for the pair to meet up on arrival. Nick told everyone at work he was off for a quick trip to Spain and arrived at the airport in Moscow in November 2008 alone, hoping like hell he'd have a smooth passage.

Predictably, it wasn't to be. As the only westerner checking in for the flight, he was immediately detained. Everything followed the usual pattern. They took his passport off him, then handed it to someone else while they stood and said nothing. Eventually, Nick could bear it no longer.

'What's the problem?' he asked in English, pretending he didn't speak Russian to keep the ruse that he was he was just an ordinary tourist going for an ordinary holiday. They stayed silent.

'Come on,' Nick urged. 'Look, I'm going to miss my flight if you don't hurry up.'

Finally, a security officer arrived and guided Nick into a small room. 'Where are you going?' he asked.

'Yerevan,' Nick replied, citing the Armenian capital.

'Why?' asked the officer.

'Tourism,' Nick said.

'Where are you going?' the man repeated.

'Yerevan.'

'Why?'

'Tourism.'

After a good few rounds, Nick broke. This approach wasn't working at all. He started speaking in Russian, and deepened his voice and adopted a much more brusque and curt tone to make it sound more authentic.

'Look, I've got a Georgian friend I play rugby with,' Nick said in Russian, noting that the officer didn't so much as blink to hear the abrupt change of language. 'I'm going there to meet him and his dad to watch a rugby game. It's my holiday.'

The officer looked at him. 'So how much money do you have?'

Nick sighed; he really didn't want to lose his money again, like the last time he'd been at the airport. Then he had an idea, and emptied all the money from his wallet and laid it out on the desk between them. He knew that would make the officer panic. If someone were to walk in, they'd see the money and assume he was taking a bribe. It did the trick.

'Put your money away,' the man snapped. 'Look, here's your passport. Now you go and catch your flight.'

Nick boarded the plane at the very last minute before it was due to take off. Three and half hours later, he arrived at Yerevan Airport and watched as all his fellow passengers disappeared into the night, catching buses to the city. He was left there, alone, waiting for his next flight, due to leave at 7am the next morning. He settled into a chair and tried to make himself comfortable, but an airport official came up and tapped him on the shoulder.

'What are you doing here?' she asked him. 'The airport is closing now for the night.'

'I've got a flight early tomorrow to Georgia,' Nick said in Russian. 'Is it all right if I stay here?'

She looked doubtful. 'I am sorry, my Russian is not very good,' she told Nick, and then lifted her handset and talked to someone in Armenian. After she'd finished, she said to Nick, 'Do you speak English?'

He smiled. 'I am English,' he said.

'Well, why did you not say so?' she asked him. 'Why did you talk to me in Russian?'

'I thought you'd understand Russian,' Nick said.

'But no, you're not in Moscow now,' she chided him. 'Don't insult me. I am Armenian, not Russian. We speak English here.'

Her attitude had otherwise completely changed, however, hearing Nick was English, and she arranged for the bar to be reopened and for Nick to be given food and drink, and to be looked after for the rest of the night.

Nick caught the flight the next morning and went into Tbilisi to meet up with Giorgi and see all the plans that were being drawn up for the country's first casino. Everyone was so relaxed and friendly, Nick thought he'd actually enjoy living in Georgia.

'Georgians,' says Nick now, 'are honestly the nicest people in the world. They are lovely. And I thought that boded well if I was going to go and live in Georgia for the next few years.'

After going through all the charts with the managers on the project, arrangements were made for Nick to be driven to Batumi, the designated site on the Black Sea, to meet President Saakashvili. On the five-and-a-half-hour drive there, Giorgi briefed him. Apparently, the President was paranoid that the Russians planned to kill him, and surrounded himself with tight security everywhere he went. Everyone, as a consequence, had to be careful, with no sudden movements, as the security detail was known to be extremely jittery, and would shoot first, and ask questions later. It was set to be an historic day, however. Saakashvili was going to hold the country's first-ever live televised meeting on the rooftop of the building set to become the casino, with a select group of politicians, to announce officially the multi-billion-dollar project.

The next morning, Nick and Giorgi made their way to there. As they stood on the building site, Giorgi pointed out all the snipers on the cranes surrounding the area. Then, four black Hummers drove up, reversed and spun around so they were facing out again. Suddenly, the whole scene was swarming with Georgian security guards dressed in black with mirrored sunglasses, chewing toothpicks, and armed to the teeth.

'This is ridiculous!' Nick whispered to Giorgi. 'It's like they've all seen a Hollywood movie about what security should look like.'

Giorgi paled. 'No, Nick,' he said. 'Say nothing!'

'But this is crazy,' Nick argued.

'Nick, Nick, shut up,' Giorgi pleaded. 'It's said they can all lipread – and in seven languages.'

Then the politicians started walking in through the gates and Giorgi told Nick each of their names and their ministries. But Nick's attention was elsewhere. As the gates were opened for each new arrival, he'd just seen a battery of TV crews outside, setting up their cameras. From their jackets and the signs on their equipment, he could see one was from Channel One Russia, the major national Russian TV broadcaster, and another was from RT, the Russian state-controlled international news TV network.

Immediately, the smile froze on Nick's face, and he could feel his hands start to shake. He could just imagine Shuvalov sitting at home, and turning on his TV to see Nick shaking hands with the Georgian President when he was supposed to be 6000 kilometres away, basking in the sun on the Costa del Sol.

# SEVEN

# GEORGIA ON MY MIND

**FOR A FEW SECONDS,** Nick stood fixed to the spot, panic-stricken. He looked around him. Every muscle in his body was urging him to bolt, but he knew any sudden movement would attract the unwelcome attention of the horde of security guards. The TV crews were setting up their cameras and were busy focusing them on the scene in front of them – and he would be centre-frame.

Giorgi was looking at him curiously. 'Are you okay, Nick?' he asked.

'No, no, I'm not,' Nick hissed back. 'I can't be here. I've got to get out of here. I'm not meant to be here. I told Shuvalov I was in Spain.' He expected Giorgi to tell him not to worry, that it would all be okay. But Giorgi didn't.

Instead, he looked around and frowned. 'Yes, you've got to go!' he said, his voice low and urgent. 'Walk slowly with me towards that other exit. The cameras won't be able to follow us there.'

He set off at an unhurried, steady pace and Nick followed him, feeling his heart was beating so loudly that he couldn't believe others wouldn't hear it. As they reached the exit gate, Giorgi opened it carefully so as not to make any noise and the pair slipped out. But they hadn't escaped the notice of the guards. As they crossed the car park, still trying to keep to the same relaxed stride, five of them came out of the same exit and ran after them, waving their guns in the air and shouting at them to halt. Giorgi turned around to face them.

'It's okay,' he shouted in English. 'We're tourists! We're tourists!'

The men looked unsure, conferred in Georgian, then nodded, lowered their guns and sloped off.

'What did you say that for?' Nick asked his mate.

'Nick, they're not stupid,' he replied. 'They won't shoot a tourist. Now let's get out of here. And you can meet President Saakashvili another time.'

As they walked past shops in the town, one had a TV set on in the window. They paused in front of it and could see the President holding court against the background they'd just been occupying. Nick had never felt more relieved in his life.

He now wanted to get out of Georgia as soon as possible, realising how easy it was to have his cover blown. He told Giorgi to pass on to Saakashvili's office that he'd accept the job, as soon as the Moscow project was completed, probably in a few months. His friend was delighted. 'It will be so good to have you here,' he told him. 'And I think Luda and the children will love it here, too. It is such a different life to Russia.'

The pair agreed he'd meet the President and his staff when he'd finished his work in Moscow and was ready to return to Georgia but, for now, Nick was keen to return to Russia, where, on arrival, he silently congratulated himself. He'd managed to avoid detection and Georgia beckoned as a great place to live for the family, with an excellent, long-running project to work on that would lead to even bigger and better jobs in the future. There was only one more hurdle to cross: an interview with a prominent, and extremely powerful, Georgian in Moscow to win his approval.

The day he went to his office to meet this man is forever seared on Nick's memory. He'd dressed up in his smartest suit and tie but couldn't erase a niggling worry at the back of his mind: the address he'd been given was strangely familiar. As he got out of the car, he suddenly realised why. The office was right next door to the premises of one of his bosses on the Shuvalov work site. He walked as fast as he could, with his face down, hoping against hope his own boss wouldn't unexpectedly appear and ask him what he was doing there.

But luck was on his side, and he made it to the Georgian's office apparently undetected. It was a shock to walk in, however. Behind the solid, anonymous door, the property opened up into a veritable palace, with chandeliers, marble and what looked like gold-layered fittings. Immediately, Nick felt even more uneasy as he was searched, then ushered into the inner sanctum to meet the man who now had the final say over his future.

'I didn't like it,' Nick says. 'I felt really nervous. I didn't know how to behave, either. Should I come over as kind of tough and strict, or just normal? I just felt totally out of my depth. This was someone with a reputation for being a formidable player in Russian, and Georgian, politics and I didn't know whose side he was really on. I found it a very difficult meeting, but I must have done okay. At the end of it, he said I could have the job.'

Nick went straight home, told Luda that it looked as though they could soon be in Georgia and changed into his normal clothes to go back to work. The children were off school that day, and they looked puzzled as to why their parents were wreathed in smiles and kept hugging them, and then each other.

'What's happening?' asked Michael, by then eight years old.

'Oh, nothing, mate,' Nick told him. 'I'm just happy to be home and to have such a wonderful wife and kids.'

'But something must have happened since this morning,' Michael persisted. 'You had us this morning too and you didn't look like that then. Ever since you came back from Spain, you've been grumpy.'

Nick grinned. 'We've just had some good news, but I'll tell you about it some other day. Now, don't you have some homework to do?'

Nick set off for work, reminding himself not to look upbeat to avoid raising suspicions. The Client's project was about seventy-five per cent done, so he'd only be a few months more in Russia. It wouldn't do to be found out so close to leaving. That day passed without incident but, just as Nick was preparing to leave for home, the manager he was most friendly with suggested they go for a quick drink at the bar over the road. Nick said he wanted to get home, but his friend wouldn't take no for an answer.

As soon as they walked into the bar, with its blaring music and its noisy clientele all talking at the top of their voices, his friend leaned towards him. 'Don't speak,' he hissed. 'Don't speak any more in the offices. They've been bugged.'

Nick felt alarmed. 'Are you sure?' he whispered back. 'How do you know?'

The man said another colleague's name who'd been berated by their boss, who'd been able to repeat, word for word, a conversation the colleague had had in the office the day before. 'They knew everything,' Nick's friend said. '*Everything.*'

Nick was already aware that all the phones on site, as well as everyone's mobile phone, were being monitored by the estate's security office, but this was new. This had never occurred to him before. He'd always been extremely careful, however, never to confide his movements to anyone he worked with, so felt sure he'd be okay.

Looking back, however, it felt like that was the moment everything started to turn.

In parliament, constitutional amendments were passed on the last day of that year, 2008, to extend the terms of the president and parliament. It meant any president who won the next election in 2012 would be able to serve six years in office, rather than four. With Putin installed as Prime Minister, he'd be eligible to run for president again and, if he were elected, serve for longer.

When Nick had originally worked in Russia, he'd been able to go in on a one-year, multi-entry visa, but now that regulation had been changed due to a new frostiness in relations with Britain. In late 2004, the former Russian military intelligence officer Sergei Skripal had been unmasked as a double agent, acting for the UK; he'd been arrested by the FSB, tried and convicted of high treason, and jailed for thirteen years. The ongoing rows between the two countries, with tensions exacerbated by the poisoning in London of Alexander Litvinenko, meant Russia retaliated against UK citizens, allowing them to be issued with visas that were valid for only three months. As a result, Nick had to travel back to the UK every quarter with the children, who were also on British passports, to collect fresh visas in London. He'd usually take Luda with them to turn the trip into a family holiday. The children would catch up with their grandparents, drink milk – there was no fresh milk in Russia back then – and eat some of their favourite foods.

'The first thing we'd all do when we arrived was to have a drink of milk and a sausage roll,' Nick laughs. 'I also loved going to an English pub and hearing everyone talking and joking in English as I hadn't heard, or spoken in, English for so long. I remember once going into a betting shop and putting a couple of quid on Manchester United to win the next day. I don't normally gamble but I thought I'd put some money on something just because I could. And I spent an hour talking to the person behind the counter as it was such a novelty talking in English.

'Another time, we were only there for a day as that's all the time it would take to get the visas. So, I asked Michael and Anya, "What do you want to eat today – Indian, Chinese or fish and chips?" And Anya said, "All of them!" So that's what we did; we had a Chinese meal, then an Indian, then went to a fish and chip shop. We ate so much that day. And when we got on the Aeroflot flight to Moscow, Anya threw up everywhere. It went absolutely everywhere. And that was everything she'd eaten that day.'

While that wasn't Anya's favourite memory of returning, she generally loved the trips. 'We used to like going back and seeing Nan and Grandad,' she says. 'We'd have Skype calls with them every once in a while, and Nan would send us presents in the post, mostly English food we missed, like Paxo stuffing, but it was nicer to see them in person.'

Michael enjoyed going back to England, too. 'One time, we went back for Christmas,' he says. 'I remember Nan gave me a cuddly toy, a blue bear. It was always my favourite. Then when we returned to Russia, my parents bought me a little furry cat, which I called Vasya, which is Russian for 'royal'. But we always liked visiting. There were a lot more things in the shops in England and it was great to eat different food and go to new places. I had an atlas, that was one of my favourite books, so I could see where we were in the world.'

This time, when Nick told his bosses he was having to return to London to renew his visa, they said that would be fine, but he would be going alone with his children. 'Your wife stays here,' said one of The Client's people.

'No, we want to go together, like we always do,' Nick argued.

The man shook his head. 'You will be going without her.'

'But why?' Nick asked.

'You know why,' the man frowned. 'You will do what I say . . . or face the consequences. Understood?' Then he turned on his heel and left.

Nick was stunned. 'When someone in his position says something like that, then you know exactly what the score is. There's nothing you can do about it. It then started to occur to me that my life was being completely controlled by the Russians. They decided if I could have a visa. They decided who could leave. Even when once I went back to London and I didn't have enough clear pages in my passport for the visa, I phoned the office and said I'd be delayed by a few days. Someone immediately called back and said it had been sorted, and I was now fine to get the visa and travel that day. The Russians had fingers in every pie, and they were used to getting their own way. What they said, went.'

Soon after, Nick noticed his name was being taken off a lot of the official documents, and he was being denied access to many of the areas of The Client's business, and life, that he'd previously been involved with before. His sense of unease only mounted.

'I started to think that Russian security had found out about me going to Georgia,' Nick says. 'I don't know how they found out, but they had so many means, and people, at their disposal. They just didn't seem to trust me anymore. While I noticed their paranoia around me, I began feeling paranoid too. It just all feeds each other. I think I knew so much about their affairs, and they were angry that I'd visited Georgia and they were scared what I might do with all the information I had. So, they started to flex their muscles to show me how much power they wielded over me. And it started to get quite scary.'

It wasn't helped either by more mysterious deaths of people who'd been disobedient or critical of the regime. In January 2009, human rights lawyer and Putin critic Stanislav Markelov was shot dead by a masked gunman close to the Kremlin. He'd represented Politkovskaya as well as the editor of an opposition newspaper and Chechen torture victims. A journalist, Anastasia Baburova, who was at the scene and tried to help him, was also shot.

Six months later, in July 2009, another human rights activist, Natalya Estemirova, was abducted from her home in Chechnya; her body was later found nearby, with gunshot wounds to the head and chest. The organiser of a vigil held in Moscow for her nine days later was arrested. The murderer has never been caught.

Such events made Nick even more nervous, and he and Luda discussed their position often. They were always careful to have such conversations well out of Michael and Anya's earshot, though. They couldn't afford to risk either of the children innocently mentioning some sensitive piece of information to one of their friends in the playground, and that information reaching the ears of their parents, and then the ears of the people Nick worked for. It was eminently possible that their children were being deliberately targeted and befriended by the offspring of some of The Client's workers, too. Nothing could be ruled out.

'It was so stressful for Luda, as well,' Nick says. 'We were having so many difficulties with the visas and making her stay in Russia was so hard. She always had this terrible fear that maybe me and the children wouldn't come back. I'd obviously reassure her, but it was horrible for her, watching us leave. There were always lots of tears at the airport when we all said goodbye. And then I'd worry that maybe one day we wouldn't be allowed back into Russia, so it was a huge strain on us all.'

Shuvalov, meanwhile, was only cementing his power in government, with an announcement in December that he'd be heading the organising committee for Russia to host the FIFA World Cup in 2018 in competition with England, Belgium, Holland, Spain and Portugal. Then, early in January 2010, just as his winter garden project neared completion and Georgia was looking more attractive than ever to Nick, the strangest thing happened. As Nick, Michael and Anya prepared to return to London again for their visas, he was told that, this time, none of them would be allowed to leave. He and Luda were distraught. Quite apart from Nick needing a new visa, they needed fresh visas for the children, too, otherwise they'd be deemed unlawful, and who knew what might happen to them in the future?

'I thought, *Is this it?*' Nick says. 'I thought, *This is really, really, really bad.* Everything seemed to be coming to a head.'

Russian specialist Associate Professor Matthew Sussex of the Australian National University's Strategic and Defence Studies Centre has seen this happen before. 'It's a fairly familiar pattern,' he says. 'When you're told not to leave Russia, then generally it's a good idea to get out straight away.'

Nick, however, was helpless to do anything but sit and wait it out. It took two months of agony, especially with the eruptions of the Icelandic volcano Eyjafjallajökull in March and April that sent a massive ash cloud over the earth, prompting twenty countries to close their airspace to commercial jet traffic. Finally, however, his boss came back to him and said Nick was now free to take his children to London to renew all their visas.

'You can go now,' he said icily. 'But if you don't come back from the UK, it won't be good for you. You know what will happen to you and your family.'

Nick didn't even like to think about that, but thanked him as politely as he could, while pointing out that they were no longer free to travel as they were now unlawful. His boss just smiled and made an appointment for him to see the Russian Immigration Minister, who, without a single question, stamped the requisite forms to make all three legal once more, and allowed them to visit London for the day for the visas.

Yet Nick just knew they couldn't continue like this. Every day, it seemed, something happened to make him fear for the worst, and it was getting harder to hide his and Luda's anxiety from the children.

Finally, the killer blow landed. He was told at work that his greatest ally, his manager friend, was being demoted. He was replaced by someone else, who, in turn, was also relieved, and then a person was appointed who everyone in the office already disliked. This third man was nicknamed The Worm because he would do anything, and everything, he was told to do, even if he knew it was practically or morally wrong. Later, Nick discovered The Worm had lost both his parents as a child and been brought up in an orphanage in Armenia where those in charge routinely picked out one child to receive extra food portions, sweets and treats, to persuade them to inform on the other kids. The Worm had been that boy. Shortly after he was promoted to his new position, he was ordered by The Client's people not to pay his former boss the 400,000 euros he was owed. He didn't argue.

What came next was a lesson in how things can go horrifyingly wrong when people feel they're being double-crossed in high-stakes situations. Nick was invited out to dinner and then taken, instead, to a meeting between the two former bosses who'd been ousted. They told him they had arranged for two members of the Militsiya to stop The Worm outside the worksite, 'find' a large amount of heroin on him, arrest him and then give him a choice: he could either pay up a large sum of money for his freedom or . . . or . . .

'That was the moment I thought that I really have to get out of Russia, and soon,' Nick says. 'I thought if these people suddenly turn on me, I don't have the contacts, or the money, to avoid what could happen to me. And anything, I now knew, could happen. And you wouldn't have any idea before it happened. I could see myself in The Worm's position, just disappearing.'

# EIGHT
# THE GREAT ESCAPE

**IF NICK HAD BEEN** plotting The Great Escape from the World War II Nazi maximum security work camp Stalag Luft III, he couldn't have planned, or prepared, any more carefully. Unlike the Allied prisoners of war, he couldn't rely on others to help him dig his tunnel. He couldn't afford to tell any other person alive, apart from Luda, of his scheme; even his children had to be clueless until it came into play.

He and Luda would talk about it only when they were in a noisy, open-air public place, where they'd whisper into each other's ears. They couldn't risk discussing it at home, where they thought they might be bugged, in any café or restaurant where there could be more listening devices planted, or on their phones in case their conversations were being listened to. They also had to make sure they could never be overheard by either Michael, now ten, nor Anya, nine, as it would be impossible to expect secrecy from such young children, and neither parent wanted to scare them by demanding it.

For the 11.5 million residents of Moscow, the year of 2010 was one to forget. The series of eruptions in Iceland continued, filling the air with ash and dust. That summer, a heatwave triggered peat fires in various regions of the country to flare up worse than ever before, blanketing Moscow in another dense smog of toxic carbon monoxide and particulates that caused more deaths in the city than the COVID-19 pandemic later would.

'What I remember most of our time in Russia were those peat fires,' Michael says today. 'The smell of chemicals in the air in Moscow was overwhelming. You just couldn't breathe outside. I remember when both happened – the volcano and the fires – you couldn't really go outside. It was too dangerous.'

If anything, these events served only to harden Nick's resolve to get out as quickly as possible and he started laying the ground-work for escape. In the office, he began talking loudly, and at every opportunity, about his desire to become a Russian citizen with a Russian passport; after all, he lived in Russia, worked in Russia and planned to stay in Russia forevermore. He didn't want all this hassle of going to Britain for visas, he'd tell anyone within earshot, when his heart lay with Russia. If only Shuvalov would sign off on him becoming a Russian!

He'd often discuss Michael and Anya with his workmates, too. 'They love school here,' he'd say, 'and their Russian is coming along nicely. They're getting a much better education here than they would back in the UK. Michael said the other day that he wants to get a job in Russia when he leaves school and Anya just loves the place. I'm so happy that they're so settled here, too.'

At least some of that was actually true. Michael was excelling at school. He'd been, like any kid, eager to blend in, but he was proving to be such an excellent student that the result was quite the opposite.

'I wanted to do the best I could, especially being a foreigner,' he says now. 'Even back then and as young as I was, I wanted to fit in as much as I could. I remember the teachers used to get very upset with me, because it's kind of weird to say, as an English kid, but I used to be top of the class in Russian language. I was very fluent, and still am. I remember one of the teachers told the entire class that she was very disappointed in them all because a foreigner could speak the language better than they could. She said it in a nasty, kind of resentful, way.'

Anya was just as settled but didn't find lessons as straight-forward as her brother. 'My English was always better than my Russian and I struggled with some of the educational stuff,' she says. 'Especially maths. I found it complicated. But I quite enjoyed doing sports and was pretty good at cross-country running. I preferred to do physical things and I was always really athletic. That was probably due to Dad being into rugby and spending a lot of time with us throwing balls and doing outdoor activities. I also liked creative activities and loved drawing animals especially.'

At home, Nick and Luda were secretly spending nearly every minute of every day trying to work out how best to get out of Russia. Georgia was their favoured location, of course, especially with the job offer Nick already had there, but the more they talked about it, the more dangerous it felt. Even if they managed to leave Russia successfully, flying to Armenia and then on to Georgia, they imagined they'd still be constantly looking over their shoulders for payback. The country was so close, geographically, and with such a big population of Russians, it just seemed too risky. Then the pair began scouring maps of Russia, looking for unstaffed borders with Ukraine or Belarus that they could drive over to make good their escape. From there, they'd keep driving through Poland to Germany, France and then onto the ferry to England. Yet England didn't feel much of a safe haven, either. There were a lot of wealthy Russians living in London, too, with considerable power and reach through the political and economic systems. They would find it easy to exact revenge on Nick and his family for his perceived betrayal.

The grinding poverty in much of Moscow was also starting to get to Nick. One of his workmates, who was also a friend and whose home Nick and the family had visited on a couple of weekends, usually arrived an hour earlier at the site. One time when Nick came into his office, he found the man fast asleep in his chair. As a joke, he kicked it to wake him up.

'What are you doing sleeping in the bloody office and in my chair?' Nick demanded with mock severity. 'Get up! Come on, get out there with the other lads!'

The man woke up with a start, saw Nick was being playful and laughed as he got up and went outside to work.

But two mornings later, Nick came in and again found him asleep behind his desk. 'Come on, Sleeping Beauty,' he said. 'What are you doing asleep here *again*?' As the man got to his feet, Nick had a sudden thought. '*Hang on, why* are *you sleeping here?*'

The man looked shamefaced. 'I'm just really tired, Nick,' he answered.

'I can see that, but I can't have you tired and then going out to work on a potentially dangerous project. Tell me, why are you so tired?'

It turned out the man's six-year-old daughter was seriously ill, but he couldn't afford the expense of a hospital bed for her. Instead, he'd made a deal with the head of the hospital: if he spent all night working in the hospital, fixing doors and beds and doing other maintenance jobs, they'd find his little girl a bed. Nick was appalled.

'But can't you pay for the bed and the treatment?' he asked the workman. 'I'm paying you good wages.'

'Of course,' the man said. 'But you're not paying that kind of money. I don't have that much.'

'How much are we talking about?' Nick asked.

'All up about US$1000.'

Nick was shocked to realise hospital care was so far out of the reach of a regular worker. 'Here,' he said, pulling out his wallet and counting out ten US$100 bills. 'Take it – and do us both a favour and get some sleep.'

'It's a very hard life for many Russians,' Nick says. 'But they are such great people when you get to know them, and they accept you. They've got good hearts but it's not fair that so many are forced to live like that.'

By contrast, the lives of the rich and powerful had to be seen to be believed. Nick had personally witnessed the luxuriously fitted-out private jets, the imported black Mercedes, the top-of-the-range jewellery, the Patek Philippe, Rolex and Chopard watches. He'd also heard all about the fabulous apartments and mansions around the world owned by the Russian oligarchs. And then there were the regular trips overseas staying in the top five-star hotels and resorts, eating at Michelin Star restaurants and drinking only the finest wines and champagnes. He'd experienced that for himself.

'It was terrible,' he says. 'To think of so much poverty, and so much wealth, existing side-by-side in the same country. It was simply obscene. Of course, there's corruption in every country, but there's so much money in Russia among so few, it's insane.'

Nick and Luda were still trying to finalise their getaway plan when, out of left field one day, came a stroke of luck. One of the bosses approached Nick and told him The Client had a massive new project he wanted undertaken in far eastern Russia – would he be interested in working on it? The project was for a conference centre and hotels and theatres to be used for the upcoming 2012 Asia-Pacific Economic Cooperation (APEC) summit in one of the two offshore areas of Russia designated Special Administrative Regions, with tax incentives introduced to lure Russian companies based in other countries to come back to the motherland. One was in the far west, on Oktyabrsky Island between Lithuania and Poland, and the other, Nick's project, was in the far east, on Russky Island 9300 kilometres east of Moscow near the borders with China and North Korea, with plans for the world's longest cable-stayed bridge to connect it to the mainland at Vladivostok.

Nick had absolutely no intention of uprooting his family to take them to such an isolated, far-flung spot, but did everything he could to persuade everyone at the company that he could never have imagined such a wonderful opportunity. He asked constantly when he and his family could go, for progress reports on what was happening over there, and who might be going with them.

'I tried to look really enthusiastic,' he says now. 'Then I started saying that I just had to nip over to the UK first to sort some stuff out and get the kids organised to go over to the far east. It was elaborate play-acting that going to the far east was a great dream of mine, and I really wanted to go there, I wanted to be a Russian and make a real contribution to the development of the country. I just wanted to convince them to let us all leave Russia and go over to the

UK together, because we would definitely, definitely be back to take up this wonderful opportunity.'

By this time, his visa was again due for renewal. He applied to leave the country with just Luda this time, to see what his bosses' attitudes would be. They agreed instantly and, at that moment, he realised he'd managed to convince them that his enthusiasm for living in Russia was genuine. He wanted to put it to one last test on a dry run, however. He applied for a UK visa for Luda and then bought them both a same-day return flight to London. At the airport in Moscow, the couple were waved through, they arrived in the UK without incident, Nick picked up his visa and they flew straight back without a hitch.

All the time this was happening, Michael and Anya had no idea that a plan was being hatched. They could see that their dad was stressed, but they put that down to problems at work.

'They were very good at hiding any tension from us,' Michael says. 'Occasionally, it'd be pretty obvious that something bad was happening. I remember one time, we were in a big shopping centre, having tea and cake, and my dad had to take a phone call and I remember seeing him being very stressed out, and very angry with whoever was on the phone. I was never sure what it was about but we just assumed it was work.'

A month later, Nick told his bosses the whole family was going on a weekend trip to England to pick up the supplies they'd need for their new life in Russia's far east. They had no objection. Nick said they'd just be a few days and, to avoid any suspicion at all, he and Luda packed just a few items of carry-on luggage.

'It was hard as we'd made so many friends in Moscow, but we couldn't risk saying goodbye to any of them,' Nick says. 'And we knew many of them we'd never see again, probably ever. But if we got caught doing this, we knew it would be the end for us, and we didn't want to get any of our friends in trouble if the authorities tried to implicate them in our escape. If we were stopped, and our plan not to go back was found out, I knew I'd be arrested on some trumped-up charges, as I'd seen happen to others, and that would be it. My life would be over.

'I've looked back many times and wondered if I'd become as paranoid as the bosses. But then you know the risks and when the stakes are so high, even a one per cent risk becomes too much.'

Nick told the children they were all going on a quick trip to London and they should bring just their very favourite things. Michael put his blue bear, Vasya the cat, a plastic toy spider, his PlayStation and his atlas in his holdall. He stacked his schoolbooks tidily in his room and laid out his PlayStation cartridges so everything would be ready for him to pack for school on the Monday morning of his return. Anya slipped some of her favourite drawings into her bag. Nick went to the local electronics market in Moscow and bought a mid-range Nikon camera, thinking it would be a good way to record whatever would be happening next.

But there was something else important Nick had to do before they left. He owned two laptops: one for work; and a personal one for all his own documents and communications. The day before, he'd copied a number of files from his work laptop to his private one, mainly concerning Shuvalov and his business affairs. Now, he went into the kitchen and slipped the private laptop out of its case, checked that the battery was completely drained, then took a screwdriver from the drawer. Carefully, he unscrewed the casing and opened it. Next, he reached in and unscrewed the hard drive from the machine, pulled it gently out, wrapped it in newspaper and put it in a manila envelope, which he tucked into his travel bag. Then, he did the same with his business laptop, but put its hard drive onto the benchtop. He looked at it for a few moments and finally reached into the same drawer to pull out a hammer, which he raised and brought crashing down on the hard drive, time and again, until it lay scattered all over the bench and the floor in smithereens. He swept all the pieces into a plastic bag, tucked it into his jacket pocket and walked around the apartment one last time, noticing, with a pang, how neatly his son had set up his room in preparation for school the next week.

Then, on Saturday 2 October 2010, with just a few small bags between them, the little family set off for their weekend to London. The children had no idea this journey was going to prove so momentous, and Nick felt he was holding his breath all the way through Moscow customs until he was safely sitting in his seat and heard the roar of the engines as the Aeroflot plane finally nosed its way into the sky. 'It was terrifying, absolutely terrifying,' Nick says. 'But the easiest way to raise suspicions at an airport is to appear terrified. So, it was very, very hard. So hard.'

It might have looked much less dramatic than crawling through a self-dug tunnel to freedom in World War II. But Nick was sure it felt just as nerve-racking.

# NINE
# HIDING OUT

IT WAS A DULL, drizzly day in London when the Stride family arrived at Heathrow in October 2010, but Nick barely noticed. He was thrilled that they'd made it out of Russia and into Britain. But there was no time for self-congratulation. As soon as they all cleared customs, he went to an airline counter, then to a hotel booking office, and rushed Luda, Michael and Anya into a black cab and dived in after them. They had a reservation at the Holiday Inn close to the airport and he was eager to get there.

After checking in, the four went up to their room, Nick drew the curtains and then sat the kids down.

'There's something we have to tell you,' he said. 'We're actually not staying in London. We're catching another flight in a couple of days to Australia.'

Michael and Anya were both open-mouthed.

'I'm not actually sure what I was thinking,' Michael says now of his ten-year-old self. 'I was excited at the thought of going to a new country that I'd seen before in my atlas, but it was more like going with the flow. As a kid, you don't question these things. What happens, happens.'

Anya, nine, was electrified by the thought of seeing some of the animals her dad had shown her pictures of, when he talked about his first trip to Australia. 'I wanted to see kangaroos and koalas and all the nature they had in Australia,' she says. 'I didn't mind that we were leaving Russia. Australia just sounded like a great adventure.'

Nick had decided early on that it would simply be too dangerous to stay in the UK. Back at that time, the capital was nicknamed 'Londongrad' because of the sheer volume of Russians who owned homes there, and used it as a base for their business dealings, with an estimated £27 billion invested in Britain. After the collapse of the Soviet Union, the budding oligarchs looked to London as a safe place to invest and enjoy their nouvelle richesse. That intensified after 1994, when the British government introduced its 'golden visa' scheme that meant anyone who could invest at least US$1.3 million, a sum that was later doubled, could live freely there.

Seven years before the Strides arrived back, oil magnate Roman Abramovich, a close friend of Putin, had caused an international sensation by moving over and buying Chelsea Football Club for a reputed US$195 million. That opened the floodgates for his countrymen, and the Russians soon became notorious in London for their astonishing wealth, their massively over-the-top conspicuous consumption, their parties, their drinking and their exceptionally poor taste.

Russian expert Associate Professor William Partlett of the University of Melbourne Law School describes that period as one of extreme closeness between the two countries. 'At that time, there was a nexus between Moscow and the Thames,' he says.

'So many oligarchs purchased properties in London, and they were constantly moving in and out. I can totally get why [Nick] would want to get further away to Australia instead.'

Another Russian authority, Dr Leonid Petrov of the Australian National University, agrees that the UK would have been too close to Russia for comfort. 'It was pretty exposed to the FSB, the secret service, military operatives, commercial interests and the Russian criminal world,' he says. 'The UK was very relaxed about who came in and came out, and money talks and corruption is always possible. After the threats they'd received, they'd have reasonable concerns and fear for their lives. I can understand why they'd want to leave the UK for Australia.'

It had been reported that Shuvalov, or his wife Olga, owned property in London, and Nick was anxious to get as far away as possible from them and all the other Russians. 'I just didn't feel safe there,' he says. 'There's no way I wanted to spend the next however many years looking over my shoulder all the time, knowing I've got my kids and family there. I thought maybe there wouldn't be much of a reaction, but I just didn't know. Russia's a different world. You can pay someone just US$200 to get someone killed in Moscow, and I didn't want to risk that. So, Australia seemed to fit the bill. It was a lot further away from Russia, and I felt we'd be safe there.'

The four spent five days in that hotel room, ordering food via room service and racing out occasionally, usually under cover of darkness, to the nearest supermarket for provisions. One night, Nick went down to the hotel skips to dispose of his plastic bag containing the fragments of his business laptop hard drive. Another day, he went out in the morning to a post office to dispatch the envelope containing his personal laptop hard drive to a secure location, the whereabouts of which he has never divulged to anyone. That, he felt, would be his insurance in case the Russians came after his family and caught up with him.

Nick didn't dare contact his parents, siblings or any of his friends in the UK to let them know what was happening. He was intent on spiriting Luda and the kids as far away as he could before breaking the news. 'The office would have expected me back at work on the Monday and when I didn't appear, I was sure they'd start making inquiries,' Nick says. 'When we didn't turn up at customs, I thought they could be out there actively looking for us. I didn't want to leave anything to chance. I'd heard of Russians slipping easily into Britain and then back out again, and I wanted to keep us totally out of sight.

'At that time, I was really unsure of the backlash of leaving The Client's people and project. They controlled my movements in and out of Russia for a long while but while I felt I hadn't done anything wrong, the fear I had was that Shuvalov never knew how much information I had about him, or what I would do with it, and would probably suspect the worst. If I was in the UK, I would always have been a threat to his name. But I thought if I moved to the furthest place from Russia, that should be enough.'

When the day of their Royal Brunei flight out of Heathrow and direct to Brisbane on 7 October arrived, Nick felt thoroughly drained. He knew he still had to keep his wits about him, however. It would be a tragedy to fail at this late stage. So, the four caught a taxi to the airport, checked in, huddled together quietly at the gate, and then finally climbed on board.

Only then did Nick allow himself to relax. And that's when it struck him: he'd been so intent this past year on planning the family's escape from Russia – the run for their lives! – he hadn't given a thought to what they'd do when they arrived in Australia. Back in Russia, he hadn't dared to imagine reaching Down Under, as so much could have gone wrong in the interim. Now, finally sitting on the plane winging its way to the other side of the world, he had to admit to himself that he had absolutely no idea.

# PART TWO
# NEW LIFE DREAMING

# TEN

# NEW LIFE DREAMING

THE MOST REMARKABLE THING about Australia when the Stride family arrived on 8 October 2010 was just how unremarkable everything was. It somehow felt so normal. The sun was shining, people were smiling and talking to one another, the colours were intense in the bright light and the air smelled as fresh as a rain shower on a hot day. It took their breath away.

After Russia, with all the pollution, the concrete high-rises, the dowdy clothing and the high drama of their escape, it was another world. The four stood outside Brisbane Airport blinking in the sunshine and beaming at one another. Nick and Luda were incredibly relieved they'd passed through customs without even a sideways glance at her Russian passport, which had invariably caused problems elsewhere, and they'd all been given six-month visitor visas, no questions asked. Michael and Anya were wide-eyed with excitement and curiosity about this new country.

'I didn't have a plan at all about what we might do now we'd made it there,' Nick says. 'It just felt wonderful to be back. It was a day I'd been dreaming about for so long. I thought if we can just live and be free and be together, then that's enough for the time being. The rest will work itself out. Of course, we knew the rules about immigration and knew we couldn't just turn up and live in another country. But I hoped the Russians would think we'd just gone home to England, and I wanted to enjoy Australia for as long as we could, away from the dangers we'd been facing, and watch Michael and Anya grow up in safety. It was such a huge relief to be there. And once we'd arrived, it was so easy to just forget about everything.'

The children were in high spirits, not only from the thrill of being somewhere so different, but also from the sugar hit on the plane. Ten-year-old Michael had discovered the button to summon the flight attendant early on and had used it frequently. 'I couldn't believe we could have free drinks and free food whenever we wanted it,' he says. 'I just kept clicking the button and saying, "Coca Cola, please!" and "Ice cream, please!" I must have done that at least ten times. You could never ask for things like that in Russia and you'd never get service like that, either. I thought I was in heaven.'

Anya, nine, was simply loving the novelty of everything that was happening. 'It had been a very long flight and I was glad we'd arrived,' she says. 'And it was so warm and sunny. I hadn't been expecting that.'

When the train to take them from the airport into the city pulled up, something even more bewildering happened. As they were waiting to get on, a man stepped off, smiled at them and said, 'G'day! Welcome to Australia!'

Michael, in particular, was incredulous. 'It was such a random thing,' he recounts. 'I remember thinking, *That's incredible: a stranger saying that to you*. No one would ever do that in Russia. No one says hello or acts in such a friendly way. Back there, you just put your head down and keep walking. You mind your own business. I thought, *Wow! Australia is already an amazing country.* And the other thing that hit me the most was that the air didn't have any smell. In Moscow, the air always smells like exhaust fumes. I thought, *Yes, this is much better than Russia.*'

They caught the train, found a cheap hotel, showered and had a quick sleep before going out again to explore the city. Nick was excited to show them around. It had been thirteen years since he'd been there but he still recognised many of the old landmarks and sights. They walked along a section of the Brisbane River, looking at some of the fancy mansions, the upmarket apartment buildings and the city skyline, and then went and ate in the city's China-town before returning to the hotel to sleep. The next morning, Nick checked how much money they had, both in cash and deposited in the HSBC Bank – a branch of which had recently opened in Moscow, allowing him to transfer his savings. They had a total of 30,000 euros, or AU\$42,000. He knew that wouldn't last them long, staying in the city, so decided they should travel around Australia, seeing as much as they could, all the while living as cheaply as possible. When their money ran out, he'd work out what they could do then.

'Okay, kids, we're going on an adventure,' he told them. 'Let's go out and buy a car and some tents and we'll head north. There's too many people down south so let's go up the coast and get as far as we can.'

Michael went with him to look at cars, while Luda and Anya wandered around the shops, goggle-eyed at the well-stocked shelves, buying provisions for the journey. Nick settled on an off-road SUV Mitsubishi Challenger. He also bought two tents and a heap of camping and fishing gear, as well as a kayak they strapped to the roof.

Their plan was to stay in Brisbane for two more nights to prepare, but the next morning, Nick's mobile rang. The sound made him jump. He didn't recognise the number on the screen but answered it anyway. The voice on the other end was Russian, male and very gruff.

'Nicholas Stride!' the man shouted in Russian. 'Where the fuck are you? You shouldn't have left! You're going to pay for this!'

Nick, taken aback and visibly shaken, hung up.

'Are you all right, Dad?' asked Anya, seeing him staring at the phone.

He quickly recovered himself. 'Yes, it's fine, darling,' he answered. 'Wrong number.' The phone immediately rang again and, this time, they both jumped.

Nick turned away from his daughter and answered it a second time. It was the same man but now he was even more enraged. He was shouting that Nick had to tell him where he'd gone and screaming profanities and threats.

'You'll pay for this with your lives!' the man yelled, finally.

Nick listened silently, then snapped the phone off. He prised open the back of the mobile, peeled out the SIM card and broke it in two, then tossed the phone back into his bag.

'I thought, *Okay, that's it,*' he says. 'No more phones, no internet, no emails. There could easily be a lot more threats against us, but I wasn't going to look. I didn't want to know. I also decided not to contact anyone, including the close friends I'd had in Russia. I wanted to make sure we didn't hear any more threats.'

Associate Professor Matthew Sussex says he's unsurprised to hear of such calls, including the death threat. 'I can see how they would have feared for their lives,' he says. 'I would have felt the same. And it's true they could have acted on those threats. They have those capabilities.'

The family left that morning, heading north, their spirits high. They drove out through the suburbs into the green rolling hills of Caboolture and then spotted the series of volcanic crags, the Glass House Mountains, signalling the start of the Sunshine Coast. They pulled off the Bruce Highway to take the coastal road, stopping here and there at some of the beautiful beaches they spotted from the car, with Nick always taking photos with his Nikon camera at every stop. At Maroochydore, they couldn't resist pulling off their shoes and socks and paddling, hand-in-hand, along the shoreline. Then they made sandwiches from the supplies they'd stashed in the car's boot and sat on the sand eating them, watching the waves break in the distance. It was everything Nick had ever hoped for.

They stopped that first night at a holiday village overlooking Sunshine Beach at Noosa, where they pitched the tents – not without difficulty – and cooked dinner over the communal BBQ facilities. It all felt very strange and exotic, but even the different insects bombarding them the moment the sun went down were fascinating.

'I was loving the experience,' Anya says. 'Everything was so different. It's all so in your face, like the big, coloured insects, the birds, the parrots, the animals. There always seemed to be something to look at. All the Australians we met on the beach or at the campsite were really nice, too. I sometimes didn't understand what they were saying, the slang words like *G'day, mate*, but everyone smiled at us. It felt good.'

As they continued up the coast, everything was just as beautiful as Nick remembered from his first visit when he drove down that same stretch of Queensland on the motorbike. Sometimes they'd stop at campsites – and they were gradually getting better at erecting the tents – and other times, ever mindful of the need to make their money go further, they'd free-camp off the roadside or in the bush. Treats, like takeaway burgers, hot chips or ice cream were rare, but no one minded. They were just happy to be together on the road in a country they were all steadily falling in love with.

'We always had a lot of fun,' Michael reminisces. 'But I did get into trouble once. I still had the plastic spider I'd brought with me from Russia and one day I thought it'd be really funny to put it in the tent and then I shouted to Dad that there was a big spider there. He came rushing over to try to get it out but soon realised it was plastic. He was very annoyed with us and threw the spider away, which I was upset about. But it was a good lesson early on not to mess about with wildlife, because it can be dangerous in Australia.'

Anya took appreciably longer to learn this fact. Thrilled that there was such a diversity of animals around– in stark contrast to Moscow's packs of stray dogs – she loved approaching anything and everything, picking up insects, climbing trees to see what would be nesting in the branches and even trying to play with snakes. One time, Luda came running out of a public toilet after seeing a black snake coiled under the lid. Anya went running towards it just as fast, wanting to get a closer look, until her dad caught up and stopped her.

Another favourite stopping point was Lake Monduran, just north of Gin Gin, in the rural bushland and cattle country of the Bundaberg region. Well known for having some of the best barramundi fishing in Australia, and home to the world-record barra catch at 44.6kg, it seemed the perfect place to try out the family's newly acquired fishing gear.

The lake was also teeming with bass and catfish and, while all around them others were hauling in great barra catches, Nick managed to hook only one fish: a catfish. As it was the first fish they'd ever caught in Australia, they decided to eat it that evening as part of a celebratory dinner, barbecuing it over their small gas stove set up on their wooden folding table. It wasn't a great success. During cooking, the oil from the fish overflowed onto the table and left a big black scorch mark that was forevermore a reminder of its muddy taste and bones. There was a reason, they found out later, why catfish are generally soaked in milk before cooking – and even then some people suggest putting them in a pan with a rock, cooking for ten minutes, then throwing away the catfish and eating the rock. 'We couldn't finish the fish,' says Michael. 'But I do remember the fishing being a really fun experience.'

When they hit the next town, they couldn't help hearing the latest sports news: Shuvalov's presentation to FIFA with regards to hosting the World Cup had won him a new round of admirers in the west. In a secret ballot, FIFA's Congress had voted Russia should stage the tournament in 2018. To keep their minds off Russia, the family decided to have a longer, three-day stop for Christmas 2010 at Seaforth, forty-five kilometres north of Mackay, and try their hand at camping on sand. With a five-kilometre-long beach, curving from Seaforth Creek to Finlayson Point, it seemed the perfect place to experiment. The children had once waded into the water at a beach in Southampton on one of their trips, but had retreated hastily from the cold water and complained the stones underfoot hurt their feet. This was an entirely different experience.

For a start, there were blue-black, red-headed brush turkeys wandering around under the trees that the dunes backed onto. Anya, ever fascinated by all kinds of animals, was entranced. Then there was the creek that Michael imagined would be full of snapping crocodiles, until he was reassured that it wasn't. But they loved the beach. 'The sand and the water were both so nice,' Michael says. 'In Southampton, the beach was all stones, and it was cold and miserable. But Seaforth was great. We all loved it, and we went fishing there and also learnt to swim.'

Nick encouraged both children to go into the water – the first time they'd really been in the sea to any depth. 'I thought it'd be safe as the water there was calm, and they had a netted area to keep the sharks away,' he says. 'But as I was watching them splash around in the water, I suddenly realised, *Jesus! They can't swim!*'

He then went in, too, and taught them, one at a time, how to stay afloat and then how to swim freestyle. 'They took to it really well,' Nick says. 'As soon as they'd got the hang of it, we couldn't get them out of the water. They'd have races too and Anya usually won. She was a natural.' Now they were competent in the water, they tried out their kayak, too.

Further north, they had another leisurely stay at the palm-fringed, fourteen-kilometre Mission Beach. Again, they camped on the beach and, whenever they managed to catch fish – any fish except catfish – they descaled them and cooked them over fires they built set in rings of rocks, or sometimes over the gas stove. It felt like bliss.

Only a week later, however, on 3 February 2011, when they were driving further north towards Cairns, Cyclone Yasi made landfall, and right where they'd been camping. The largest and most powerful cyclone seen on the eastern coast of Australia since 1918, the category five system devastated Mission Beach, where wind gusts reached to 295km/h and caused an estimated $3.5 billion in damage.

'We listened to ABC Radio wherever we were, and actually thought about driving back to Mission Beach to see if we could do anything to help,' Nick says. 'In the end, it seemed like we wouldn't be able to make much of a difference as the impact had been so great. But we were keen to give back to Australia. This country had given us a refuge when we'd needed it most and a fresh lease on life, and we were very grateful. While we had good luck, and had good weather all the way through, we were aware that could change at any moment. It seemed such a crazy country. You'd have drought in one area, floods in another, and fires somewhere else, all at the same time.'

They drove up to Cooktown, spent a few days there, then came back down, passing back through Mission Beach, in shock at its dramatic transformation, en route to Townsville, before turning inland. At Cloncurry, just before Mount Isa, they hired a metal detector to prospect for gold, but turned up only quartz and iron. They nearly came a cropper, too, when they tried to drive across a muddy path and started sinking. At one point, they considered signalling for help by setting fire to the spare tyre but eventually managed to get out by jacking up the car and using a few nearby fence posts to place under the wheels. Close by, Nick showed the family Mount Isa, which he remembered so well from his last visit, and then they drove down to the beautiful little outback town of Winton. Anya was transfixed by the wild camels wandering around the countryside. As Nick took photos, they all marvelled at the difference in the scenery compared to the coast.

'One of the great things about Australia is that, no matter where you go, it's going to be different from where you've been twenty kilometres away,' Michael says. 'In the outback, it might look a bit the same, but you'll see different rock formations, different sand, different bushes. We'd sometimes go off road, but we didn't take too many risks as we didn't know the place well enough.'

They dropped into Tennant Creek and drove south to see the Devils Marbles, or Karlu Karlu, with piles of huge, precariously balanced granite boulders scattered across the valley. Then they headed north again, stopping off at Katherine and its stunning gorge and, much to everyone's delight, saw kangaroos in the wild for the first time, and, finally, reached Darwin.

Nick loved being back at a place he'd got to know so well during his first trip, but everyone else was less keen as they found it almost insufferably hot, humid and congested. But they liked the fishing. One evening they went shark-fishing on a beach, with the rod stuck into the ground and the line heavily baited with mackerel. They sat back on the sand and relaxed but, seconds later, the rod had vanished.

'It was an expensive rod, so Dad was pretty upset,' Michael says. 'But the next morning, at low tide, we went onto the jetty there and looked out and I saw something sparkling in the distance that I thought could be our rod. We went out there and, yes! It was the rod, with the line wound around the rocks. We'd obviously caught our first shark, but it had eventually managed to collect the bait and free itself. So, I guess you can't really call that a catch.'

But Nick's mind was, by now, on other things. They had only a few weeks left on their six-month visas, their money was beginning to dwindle, and he was reluctantly having to start thinking about what their next move should be. He knew that the Russians could still be nursing a grudge against him and be worrying about what he might do next. On the other hand, it wouldn't do to overstay their Australian visas.

'As we were driving around, I kept thinking that we couldn't go back to Russia and we couldn't even return to the UK, as both would be too dangerous,' he says. 'Then again, Australia is a very sparsely populated country, and the outback is a completely different world. It could often be so barren and offer so much solitude. It occurred to me that you could be in any part of Australia, and even the Australians wouldn't know where you were. It was a thought I couldn't shake.'

# ELEVEN
# FALLING IN LOVE AGAIN

THE EMPTINESS AND WILDNESS of Australia really hit home to the little family as they continued their travels, south down to the Litchfield National Park and its waterfalls, rock holes for swimming, walking trails and towering termite mounds, and then further to Adelaide River and its famous jumping crocodiles. As they turned west, to pass through Kununurra, Halls Creek and Fitzroy Crossing, they again marvelled at the isolation of much of the outback until they hit the West Australian coast at Derby and then Broome and found more of the same.

'I saw the isolation as really kind of inspiring and different,' Nick says. 'It was just so striking. But we were sort of running out of both money and time, so I knew we'd have to hurry up. I thought maybe we should aim for Perth. When we were there, we would go to immigration, turn ourselves in and hope for the best. The very thought made me nervous, but I thought we'd go in, tell them what had happened to us, and just see what the score might be. We'd all fallen in love with Australia and Australians and thought . . . maybe . . . maybe . . . they'd let us stay.'

Indeed, they believed they were starting to assimilate to Australian culture. Although they'd started out nervous and edgy in company and suspicious of locals' friendliness, they'd gradually accepted that this was the way of life on this side of the world. No one seemed remotely distrustful when they came across a British man with a Russian wife, a son with a Russian accent and a daughter with a much more English lilt to her voice. Instead, they invariably tried to strike up conversations with Nick about cricket and, even though he hadn't the slightest interest in the sport, he made sure to read up on what was happening and find out what these mysterious Ashes were, so he could hold up his side of the banter. It took him a while to regain his fluency in English, too, after spending so many years speaking Russian, while Luda was becoming much more proficient at her new language. When they were away from their campsite one day and strong winds flattened their tents, they hid their amazement at how someone – a stranger – had put them back up for them, rather than stealing all their possessions as they felt sure would have happened in Russia.

They tried snorkelling, too, at Coral Bay, just south of Exmouth, and Michael loved it. 'The water is so shallow and warmed by the sun, it's like being in a bath,' he says. 'And the number of fish and colours of the coral are amazing. You start at one place and the currents carry you out to sea. I remember getting stung almost to death by jellyfish, but it was worth it.'

Before reaching Perth, they allowed themselves one last stop at Shark Bay, 820 kilometres north of Perth and just south of Exmouth. Within a World Heritage Site boasting two bays and stunning scenery, and teeming with wildlife, they went bush-walking, marvelling at the wild parrots, gulls, cormorants, wrens, fairy terns, ospreys, kestrels and the ungainly emus that strode across their path. They also went reptile-spotting, looking for bobtails, monitors and thorny devils. A wildlife cruise was another highlight, as they spied bottlenose dolphins, rays, turtles and dugongs. Then they took out a boat on their own to go fishing and later took turns skimming across the water in their kayak.

'When we were on our way to Shark Bay, we were driving through the bush, and I couldn't believe there'd be anything at the end of the road,' Michael says. 'Then suddenly we came over a hill and there was this beautiful sight of beaches and ocean on both sides. It was absolutely amazing. It was an incredible place. I thought the beaches were unlike any you'd ever see in the world. One, Shell Beach, was made up of billions of tiny shells that are said to be ten metres deep in some places.'

Another beach the family visited had a sign up saying, *Beware of the Stonefish*, with an image of the ugly rock-like creature that is the most venomous fish known to exist, with stings that can prove fatal to humans. Nick smiled, figuring that maybe one had been spotted about thirty years earlier, meaning the sign had to be erected.

Not half an hour later, an excited Anya ran up saying she'd found 'a million-year-old dinosaur-looking fish' that she'd just picked up and then put back down in the water, whereupon it had wandered away, walking on its fins over the seabed.

Nick realised immediately what she'd found – a stonefish. 'I told her she had to be careful and not pick anything up. But, of course, she hadn't known. She was only ten years old and had never seen anything like that in Moscow.'

After an otherwise blissful few days, they tore themselves away from Shark Bay and made for Perth, selling some of their gear along the way to raise money to keep going. But when they reached the city, it felt like a shock, so they drove 170 kilometres south to the much smaller coastal city of Bunbury. This, Nick thought, could be the perfect base while they sorted out their visas, close enough to Perth to explore the possibility of migrating through official channels, but far enough from the bustle of big-city life to feel relaxed.

They went to the local caravan park, paid for a campsite and pitched their tents. Nick and Luda were still in two minds about what was their best course of action. They considered staying in Bunbury illegally, lying low, getting some cash-in-hand work and seeing how they went, but they really needed to enrol Michael and Anya in school. They could have carried on travelling, but they were close to broke. And then there was that third option: talking to the immigration department.

Finally, the day before their visas were due to expire on 6 March 2011, Nick drove the family back to Perth, and the four of them walked, hearts in their mouths, into the offices of the Department of Immigration and Citizenship (DIAC).

At first, things couldn't have gone better. They were seen by a new compliance officer who asked them about their story, made some notes about their time in Russia, sympathised with them about the dangers of their situation, and looked alarmed about the threats they'd received. After about an hour in the office, he delivered his verdict. 'I think it'd be best if you applied for political asylum,' he said. 'That would really fit with your circumstances. Now, I'll give you the forms to fill in.'

A wave of relief swept over Nick. This sounded like the answer to all their problems. 'Does that mean we'd then be allowed to stay?' he asked.

'Yes,' replied the man. 'Now, I don't make that decision, but it would seem to me that this would be the best way forward for you.'

He handed over the forms, and Nick and Luda started filling them in. As they did so, the officer shook his head in amazement at their case. 'I can't believe I'm talking English to asylum seekers,' he said. 'We usually have to get interpreters in to speak Farsi or Arabic or Tamil, but we've never had English before . . . this is the first time I've encountered this.'

Nick smiled back at him. 'He'd made us feel really confident,' he says. 'He'd been really listening to us and was so upbeat. It was great.'

With everything now looking so rosy, Nick and Luda drove the children back to Bunbury feeling optimistic about their future. A few days later, they received a call informing them they'd been granted a two-week bridging visa to stay in the country. It didn't sound much, but Nick assumed it would be extended as soon as the department had reviewed their case. They then started making arrangements for their new life.

It was hard going, but they assumed the difficulties would be temporary. They were almost out of money by now, and sold the car to raise some more, but their visa didn't allow them to work, so they had no way of earning extra. They weren't entitled to Medicare either, so they began to live in fear of ever getting sick. Nick managed to get some cash-in-hand work helping someone mow lawns but was always terrified of the authorities discovering the breach and cancelling their visas.

One day, they ran out of both money and food. Nick remembers staring at the tube of toothpaste in the corner of his tent, wondering if it was edible. Instead, he begged the mowing contractor for a few more lawns to mow, which allowed the family to eat that evening. But Nick realised this way of living wasn't sustainable. He sat up most of that night, trying to come up with a solution. The next morning, using the cash he had left, he bought an A3 printer and some paper. Luda was confused but Nick reassured her. He then spent three hours printing out some of the best photographs he'd taken with his Nikon during their travels.

The next morning, a Saturday, the family caught a bus to the tourist attraction Busselton Jetty, fifty kilometres south of Bunbury. Nick set up a small table, on which he laid out his photos of waterfalls, beaches, sunrises, sunsets, dolphins, rock waterholes and cliffs. Within an hour, he'd sold sixteen photographs for a total of $300. 'I thought, *Wow!* I can actually earn money from photography, contrary to what my dad had told me all those years before,' Nick says. 'So, then I started printing out more photos and we went to markets and other places where tourists and locals would congregate. People were just amazed by some of the photos, and we were just lucky we'd been to so many places, and I'd taken pictures wherever we'd been. Of course, it was unlawful because we didn't have a work visa, but how else could we – or anyone else in the same position – survive? Especially when you have a family to look after.'

Two weeks later, the family returned to Perth to have their visas renewed. They were told they were going to receive only another fourteen days. Nick tried to press them for a longer period, but the office refused. It was the first indication that perhaps the process wasn't going to be as smooth as their first contact had suggested.

On the plus side, the owner of the caravan park seemed to have a sense that something was wrong. Saying he didn't like seeing a family with children living in tents when they obviously weren't on holiday, he offered them a caravan with a small annex outside for the same price as their campsite. Nick accepted gratefully. At least their new lodging felt just a touch more permanent.

Encouraged, he and Luda then enrolled Michael, now eleven, and Anya, ten, in the nearest school in Bunbury, as they were both keen to resume school and meet kids their own age. Nick anticipated that this could be a problem – and it soon was. The day after their first classes, the school office called to ask to see their passports, so Nick dropped in copies. The secretary rang again a few days later to request a copy of their visas. Nick told her he was in contact with the department and would send them shortly. He knew, however, that the fact they had short bridging visas would lead to more questions, and more complications, and the school might even insist he remove his kids from the school. So, he never did send the visas, and after a few weeks, the secretary gave up ringing him. 'I think they just put us down as really bad parents,' Nick says. 'But we knew immigration could make it difficult, so we took the path of least resistance.'

But those visas remained a constant headache. The department demanded that every two weeks the whole family travel to Perth to renew them. Nick's pleas for them to be renewed electronically were refused.

'But we don't have the money to keep coming and going to Perth,' Nick told them.

The response was abrupt: 'That's not our problem.'

Eventually, in desperation, Nick phoned the department on the morning he was expected.

'I'm sorry, we can't afford to come today,' he told them. 'If you want us, you're going to have to come and get us.' That did the trick. The next visa they were given covered them for three months.

But they were still only buying time. When Nick and Luda went in after three months to have them renewed, the department asked them where their children were.

'At school,' Nick replied. 'We can't take them out every time for this.'

The response shocked him. 'Bring them,' he was told by one officer. '*We* decide whether your children go to school or not.'

As the weeks and months dragged on with no appreciable progress in the asylum-seeker application, Nick started making more inquiries about the hold-up. And what he discovered shocked him to the core. Apparently, in the first compliance officer's excitement about meeting English speakers when Nick and Luda first arrived at the immigration office, he hadn't told them the most important thing about applying for political asylum – that they could claim free legal representation at the time of their first application. Afterwards, they could seek a pro bono legal service to help them or pay for representation by a migration agent or immigration lawyer.

Today, a spokesperson from the department confirms that, back then, 'the government-funded Immigration Advice and Application Assistance Service provided free legal assistance to all onshore asylum seekers in immigration detention and to disadvantaged protection visa applicants in the community.' *Disadvantaged* was defined as those in financial hardship with no disposable assets, or those who came from a non-English-speaking background.

Nick was devastated to learn that it was likely he would have qualified. 'But I think the more usual asylum seekers were all given in-house interpreters and those were people who knew the score and would immediately make sure their client would have a lawyer,' Nick says now. 'But the difficulty with us was that, firstly, we spoke English and, secondly, we just didn't fit into any of the usual immigration case boxes. Later on, one day, I had a phone call from someone in the Department's head office in Melbourne asking why we had no legal representation and saying we were the only current refugee applicants without representation. They could hardly believe it either.'

Nilesh Nandan is Special Counsel at MyVisa Immigration Law Advisory, one of Australia's leading immigration law firms. After reviewing Nick's case he explains that being unrepresented would have undoubtedly caused great difficulties for Nick and his family. 'All asylum seekers face a very complex journey through the legal process,' he says. 'A 2022 UNSW study by Dr Daniel Ghezelbash analysed over 6700 applications for review of unfavourable visa decisions and found that having legal representation increased an applicant's chance of success by the power of seven. That's a huge 700 per cent differential.'

At the time, however, Nick had no idea about any of that. 'We never realised that we should have insisted on legal representation that first time,' he says. 'Later, we tried so hard to find a lawyer that might act for us pro bono but every single one we approached asked where we were from and when I said the UK, they said they didn't work for people on a UK passport. Again, we just didn't fit the image of the regular refugee. The only avenue left was to pay for a lawyer, and we had no money, so could never afford one. So that became a huge problem.

'That one mistake ended up costing our family so, so dearly. Not having a lawyer was actually killing us.'

# TWELVE

# STANDING UP FOR YOUR BELIEFS

**THE WORDS IN THE** letter hit Nick like a punch in the gut. After six months of waiting to hear whether he and his family would be granted protection visas as legitimate asylum seekers, he'd been growing steadily in cautious confidence. Surely it was a good sign they'd been waiting so long? If they didn't have a strong case, wouldn't they have been given a short, sharp refusal right at the outset? And hadn't they done everything they could in the interim to demonstrate they'd be a worthwhile addition to Australia? The children were excelling at school, they'd started making close friends in the community, and they'd had the chance to prove themselves solid, respectable citizens-to-be. They dared to hope it would all be over soon, and with the best-possible outcome.

When Nick returned to the caravan after shopping for groceries one day in August 2011, and noticed an envelope had been slipped under the door bearing the unmistakable logo of the Department of Immigration and Citizenship (DIAC), he took a deep breath and tore it open. As he read, he noticed his hands were trembling.

He wasn't surprised; so much rested on this. Then the words started to sink in and swim before his eyes. Their application had been rejected.

He slumped on the bench by the flimsy fold-out table around which the family's lives revolved these days and forced himself to keep reading. The notification told him he had a right to apply for a review of the decision to the Refugee Review Tribunal within twenty-eight days. Not all was lost just yet.

Nick phoned the tribunal the next morning and said he wanted to apply for a review. The person fielding the calls asked him about his visa and said it would automatically be renewed over the duration of the re-evaluation. 'And can I have working rights attached to that?' Nick asked. 'I've heard that's a possibility.'

'You'll have to ask the department for that,' came the response.

Over the next few weeks, Nick phoned the department every second day asking for those work rights. He pleaded, he reasoned, he begged. 'How can a family live if we're not allowed to work?' he asked, over and over. 'We need to work and earn money. I've got kids. How can we eat otherwise?'

Eventually, either the officers took pity on him or he simply wore them down. They granted him and Luda new bridging visas with permission to work. It was a relief, finally, to be able to earn money legally, without the constant fear of being found out and expelled from the country. That very day, he put up notices all around Bunbury advertising his services undertaking home mainte-nance, small renovations and odd jobs, all at much lower rates than competitors'. As a result, he was soon inundated with work, and he and Luda laboured together on people's homes, doing everything from tiling to painting, concreting to carpentry.

'When I was growing up, we couldn't afford to pay people to do things like that, so we had to do them ourselves,' Nick says. 'I learnt very quickly how to be handy, and Luda turned out to be pretty good, too. I think a lot of people had been overcharged in town for a long time, so we ended up really popular. We did a lot of jobs for older women who couldn't afford anyone else. But they knew we were honest, we wouldn't overcharge and we were very competent.'

Being able to earn money changed everything. Nick had hated his kids having to live in a caravan and knew how much they hated it, too. Anya says she knew they were struggling with money, but 'I started to really wish that we had things that other people had, like a proper house, and nice food. We didn't go hungry, but we were very strict on what we bought.'

A few weeks after starting working again, Nick was able to put down the rental bond on a small two-bedroom house in the cheapest part of town. It was a huge relief to be behind brick walls again, and away from a place where the only other residents had been those similarly at the end of their tether. The big setback of late had been the tribunal's refusal to overturn the department's decision on the strength of Nick's written submission. Instead, it insisted on a formal hearing, which was set down for 6 December 2011.

'That was probably one of the worst times of my life,' Nick says now. 'We had to present our case in front of one person. We were in what was actually a huge courtroom, the doors were locked and we weren't allowed to leave. It was so intimidating. Yet again I thought how hard it was not having a lawyer with us to help. No one else seemed to go in without a lawyer; just us. And we had to present our case and speak into microphones. The one thing I'll always remember from it though was the way the tribunal member listened to us, and at the end said, "You know, I can tell when someone's lying because I'm very good at what I do." I wondered what he was getting at, then he said, "I believe everything you've told me, but I have to justify my decision today to the people above me." I immediately thought, *Okay, that's fair enough, but it sounds as if we're getting the go-ahead.*'

That Christmas was the happiest Nick had ever known. He felt relaxed and optimistic, at last, about his family's future. Luda was excited at the prospect of staying in Australia. The kids were simply ecstatic and decorated their little house with tinsel and fairy lights. Nick couldn't remember a time when the four of them had laughed and joked so much and simply revelled in one another's company.

Michael, now eleven, was loving his new school, Australind Primary, where he was excelling academically. Having come from the strict Russian education system, he'd been baffled at first by the lack of discipline at his Australian school, how naughty the kids were and how the teachers didn't seem to mind, and how little homework was assigned. But he'd been top of his class in maths and English grammar – despite English being his second language – and had only just missed out on being dux of the school. Even better, he'd won a scholarship to go into a gifted and talented program in maths and philosophy in high school.

'I think the teachers found me a bit odd, and I don't blame them, really, as I would be the only one sitting bolt upright in the classroom, listening to them, and putting up my hand when I wanted to ask a question,' Michael says.

'Sometimes, the teacher would tell a joke and everyone would fall around laughing, but I'd still be sitting there, just looking at him. At one parent-teacher evening, he told Dad that he didn't think I understood the Australian sense of humour. Dad was always so protective of us and said, quick as a flash, "Maybe he just doesn't find you funny." I thought that was hilarious.

'Then, in the evening, if you were given homework, it was just about what you'd learnt in class and it would be so easy, you'd do it in ten minutes. In Russia, we'd probably have two hours of homework a day. But gradually I was coming to understand the Australian way of thinking. And the other kids seemed to like me; I think my Russianness was my main selling point. They called me a sleeper-cell agent and would ask if I was a member of the KGB or an FSB spy and was in Bunbury to steal their technology or something. They loved poking fun at me, and I enjoyed it. It was good being accepted.'

Anya was less strong academically but was presented with the school's Citizenship Award for being the politest, most considerate girl of the year. She was developing a real love of drawing, especially animals, and often created little cartoon books. Having inherited her mother's Russian good looks, she was also extremely popular with both the girls and boys in her class.

The principal of the school, Darrin Tinley, was very happy to provide a reference for both children for the department. 'I am always impressed by the way both children conduct themselves and by the respect they show their peers, staff and the school in general,' he wrote. 'They have formed strong relationships with their classmates, which has led to both of them being elected to leadership roles within the school in 2012 . . . Michael and Anya have become very important members of our school community and contribute to our school culture in a positive way.'

Michael was keen to contribute in other ways, too. In his spare time, he was a junior volunteer for the Western Australian State Emergency Service and also did Sea Cadet training. He took his tasks there very seriously – unlike many of his fellow cadets, who often treated it more as an opportunity to lark around – and as a result kept being promoted to positions of increasing responsibility.

His sister's interests were quite different. One of her favourite places was the Bunbury Wildlife Park, with all its native marsupials, birds, frogs and snakes, particularly the snakes. She visited one afternoon and was encouraged to handle a massive woma python, and then help the keeper put it away. She was spellbound. 'That's where I found my love of snakes,' she says. 'I was fascinated by them and wished and wished that I could have a pet snake.'

The family was fitting in well with the Bunbury community, too. Local police officer Steve Delane had children at the same school, with his son Liam the same age as Michael and in the Sea Cadets with him, and his daughter Bella just a year younger than Anya. As the children became close friends, they had playdates at each other's homes.

'I really liked them all,' says Delane. 'Nick was great, and full of stories. He'd come from the other side of the world and was so good to talk to about life. Luda was a lot quieter, and the language barrier didn't help, and Anya was a lot like her mum with not a lot of conversation. But Michael was very much like his dad and very talkative and open and very mature for a young fella.'

With the children now so relaxed and happy, and the renovation work with Luda going well, Nick had more time to sit back and mull over his time in Russia. Preparations had started there for the 2012 presidential elections and the incumbent, Dmitry Medvedev, who'd taken over from Putin, proposed that Putin stand again for the ruling United Russia party. Putin agreed, and offered Medvedev the chance to become prime minister, effectively arranging for a swapping of roles. Nick was appalled.

'I hated this system,' he says today. 'There were all these incredibly rich oligarchs at the top, trading with each other, and constant reports of huge amounts of corruption, and yet the health and education systems desperately needed more money and so many ordinary people had nothing. There were people in power who were milking the place for everything they could get. Inconceivable riches. It just felt so wrong, so wrong. So many other people in Russia are suffering badly because of it.'

As he continued surfing the internet for the latest news on Russia, he suddenly came across his old boss Shuvalov's name in an article by a leading American investigative journalist and author, Michael Weiss, making numerous accusations against Shuvalov and his wife. Reading carefully, Nick could see the writer really didn't have much information on Shuvalov's business affairs. Nick had far more on that computer drive he'd kept.

Russia started playing on his mind. He thought of all the people there he knew – the workmates, the friends, Luda's family; everyone and everything he'd had to leave behind because of the danger he'd found himself in. Then he thought about those threats he'd received, and the daily misery endured by so many Russians.

'I remembered once saying to Michael, "Can you stand by and watch somebody do something you believe is wrong and do nothing?" I really think you can't. If Michael or Anya came across something wrong, I hope they'd have the courage to speak out against it. So, if I didn't, I'd be a hypocrite of the first order.

How can I teach morals to my children and not do the right thing myself? I decided to try and contact Weiss and tell him what I knew and see if he'd be interested in some of the documents I had copies of.

'I thought it couldn't do any harm. After all, we were pretty confident that the tribunal was going to let us stay in Australia, well out of harm's way.'

Michael, aged six, and Anya, five, shivering through their first winter in Moscow, in 2006, at Victory Park (Park Pobedy), with displays that honour the Soviet victory in World War II.

It was a bitter winter that year and Anya and Michael cuddle up to keep warm in the snow.

Nick, 40, in his office onsite at Zarechye, on the outskirts of Moscow, in 2008, working on the winter garden project for Russian politician Igor Shuvalov, the former deputy to Vladimir Putin.

Luda, Nick, Anya, nine, and Michael, ten, in October 2010, days after fleeing from Russia to London and then to Brisbane, preparing to set off on a six-month trip around Australia.

Bunbury, Western Australia, in 2012, where Molly the dog keeps a close eye on Michael, 12, as he fishes from the beach.

Anya, 13, rescues a green sea turtle stranded on the beach at their first stop after disappearing into the Dampier Peninsula, on the remote northernmost tip of Western Australia, near the Goombaragin Eco Retreat, in November 2014.

Snakes are everywhere you look in Goombaragin, on the road, in the house, under the sofa, in the ceiling . . .

Anya's 14th birthday, January 2015, at Goombaragin is a quiet affair – no one feels they have much to celebrate.

At the family's next home, Ardyaloon, in July 2015, Anya, 14, and Michael, 15, go handlining for fish.

Michael becomes an extremely good fisherman while at Ardyaloon. He's pictured here with a prized and tasty rock cod.

The family spends their longest period of time while hiding out on the peninsula at the Burrguk community's Banana Well Getaway where Anya, now 14, indulges her love of animals.

Another successful fishing expedition at the Beagle Bay Creek while at Banana Well results in a giant Spanish mackerel for Michael and a Chinamanfish for Anya.

After the family's Nissan Patrol succumbed to the rough conditions, an Indigenous friend swapped his old, red Toyota HiLux for some fish. It wasn't a great bargain as the vehicle had no brakes or suspension, but was still a tough car and could be driven on beaches.

A huge flash bushfire heads towards the family from Middle Lagoon, threatening the getaway and their lives.

The family's vege garden at Banana Well, where snakes and all manner of venomous creatures lurk.

# THIRTEEN
# A FAMILY DIVIDED

**AS NICK WAS WAITING** to hear back from Michael Weiss, momentous things still seemed to be happening in Russia. The Legislative elections had been held and the United Russia party, with Putin as its de facto leader, had lost its big two-thirds constitutional majority but still held onto power with just under fifty per cent of the vote. Major protests had taken place in Moscow and St Petersburg alleging voter fraud and complaining about the government. Then, on 4 March 2012, Putin won back the position of president.

Nineteen days later, however, Nick's attention was yanked back to his own situation. A tattered, torn and stained departmental envelope was shoved into the letterbox bearing the scribble, 'Not known at this address'. Nick looked at it, saw that it had his and Luda's names on it above the wrong postal address, and opened it gingerly. It had indeed been intended for them, despite someone misdirecting it.

The letter, dated 13 February 2012, contained a massive blow: the tribunal had refused their application. While it found they were indeed at risk of serious harm were they to return to the UK or Russia, it declined to review the decision on the basis that the harm was not for reasons of persecution on any of the five grounds recognised in the Refugee Convention: race, religion, nationality, membership of a particular social group or political opinion. Nick's family's case fell outside those parameters.

Worse, the letter said that if they felt the verdict was wrong, they could appeal to the Federal Circuit Court – but only on a question of law and within thirty-five days of the date of the decision. Nick's heart sunk. Without a lawyer to guide them, it would be imposs-ible to run an appeal on a legal technicality, and he had no hope of raising enough money to pay for one. And because the envelope had been incorrectly addressed, the thirty-five-day deadline had elapsed two days earlier.

Nick immediately phoned the department, pointing out the error and insisting he shouldn't be made to suffer for it. He was told to come into the office. When he and Luda arrived, it was like a nightmare unfolding before their eyes. The officer in charge looked at the letter and back at them. The situation was simple, he said: Nick and the children would have to go back to the UK, while Luda would be sent back to Russia.

The couple were aghast. 'But have you not read the letter from the tribunal?' Nick said, trying to contain his fury. 'It clearly says we're at risk of serious harm if we return to the UK or Russia. How can you make a finding like that and then send us back regardless?'

'You and the children will have to return to the UK,' the official repeated, stonily. 'Your wife will have to return to Russia.'

The full implications of his words chilled Nick to the bone. All he'd ever wanted was for his family to be able to live together in peace. He loved his wife, he adored his kids. He couldn't bear the thought of any of them being separated. But this was something far worse. This would see them wrenched apart forever. He could barely fathom what this official was saying, but suddenly he felt ice-cold with dread.

'But can't you see, if you insist on sending Luda to Russia, you'll be sending her back to who knows what?' Nick pleaded, as Luda broke down in tears beside him and he reached out to put an arm around her. 'Even the Tribunal stated she would be in danger if sent back to Russia. She could be persecuted, anything. Are you not human? As soon as she goes back to Russia, she'll also lose her children, which she'll never survive. Her children will no longer have a mother. This is absolutely heartless. Surely you can't be serious?'

'You and the children will have to return to the UK,' the official said again. 'Your wife will have to return to Russia.'

Nick took a deep breath and tried to swallow his rage and terror and misery. 'But surely there's something else we can do?' he asked. 'Another avenue we can try?'

The official looked irritated. 'Well, you could apply for a Ministerial Intervention and the bridging-visa extension that goes along with it,' he eventually replied.

'Thank you,' Nick said. 'Thank you.'

Critically, however, he had no idea that just three days after he received that fateful letter from the tribunal saying his application wouldn't be reviewed because it fell outside the Refugee Convention's five grounds, a new amendment to migration law had come into effect that substantially expanded the grounds under which you could apply. It introduced the measure of 'complementary protection' for those who didn't meet the former definition of a refugee but who nonetheless faced real and serious dangers. Not having a lawyer, Nick was totally oblivious to that development, and filled out the paperwork for the Ministerial Intervention on the previous grounds, rather than on the new grounds that could have given him a much greater chance of success. He could, in fact, have started the whole process again and in a way that would have been much more likely to have led to a favourable outcome.

'That would have been a real sliding-doors moment for Nick,' says leading immigration lawyer Nilesh Nandan. 'Few advisors properly understood the idea of complementary protection when it was first introduced into Australian Immigration law. Migration agents, lawyers and tribunal members were all still on their complementary protection trainer wheels at that time. Nick had no chance being un-represented. And it wasn't for the decision-makers to make Nick's case for him. They just don't do that. [But] if Nick's case was run properly, prospects for his success would have vastly improved.'

Yet all this was moot for Nick, who was confronted by the terrible prospect of his family being torn apart.

He submitted his application on 11 April 2012 to the Minister for Immigration and Citizenship, Chris Bowen, an appointee of Labor Prime Minister Julia Gillard. It arrived at his office in the middle of one of Australian politics' most turbulent times, during which neither of the major parties was setting new benchmarks for the compassionate treatment of asylum seekers.

The attitude in Canberra during that period was largely hard-nosed. In 2007, the Liberals' long-serving Prime Minister John Howard was finally defeated at the polls by Labor's Kevin Rudd, who, in turn, was ousted in a party-room coup by Gillard in 2010.

Everyone's hold on power felt tenuous, and to varying degrees hard-line immigration politics was the game they were all playing to try to cement their popularity with the Australian public – and elements of their own parties.

Howard had started it back in 2001 with an election victory widely credited to the turning away of hundreds of people seeking asylum who'd been rescued from an ailing Indonesian fishing boat by the Norwegian ship the MV *Tampa*. That 'Tampa Crisis' and some months later, the Children Overboard affair (with claims by Howard ministers, later proven to be false, that another group of asylum seekers had cynically thrown their own children into the water as a rescue plan) became the catalyst for Howard's new border-protection policies.

These policies were proving popular in the context of a fresh wave of boats carrying unauthorised migrants to the country – over 50,000 people in more than 840 boats – from 2008, with the majority arriving in 2012 and 2013. Gradually, stoked by various forces, the political hysteria over boatpeople and people smuggling reached unprecedented levels. Consequently, many new migrants, and would-be migrants, to Australia were viewed with widespread antipathy as politicians vied to appear as tough and ruthless in their approach to immigration as they possibly could.

Nick feared the worst – and with good reason. In June 2012, Bowen refused to intervene in Nick's case. Nick and Luda went back into the department, where they were slammed with exactly that same mantra as before: 'You and the children will have to return to the UK. Your wife will have to return to Russia.'

Luda was again inconsolable; she broke down and cried nonstop for days. Frantic with worry, he took her to the local GP. The doctor examined her and talked to her, and then wrote a report, saying she was suffering from anxiety and was a high suicide risk. Nick made sure to pass a copy on to the department, but it didn't seem to make any difference. What's more, his working rights were now set to be stripped away, and there was the possibility that Michael and Anya would be removed from school. Nick needed all his strength to keep going.

The only option, it seemed, was to make another application for a Ministerial Intervention, so Nick got busy preparing that. He was writing it the day a close friend called around. His dog had given birth to a big litter of pups, all of which he'd managed to sell except one, a gangly, black Great Dane/mastiff/Labrador cross.

'I was just wondering,' the friend said, standing in the doorway of their little house, 'you wouldn't want a dog, would you?'

Nick looked at the mutt, which was sniffing Nick's feet. He could see that, even at just a few weeks old, she had massive paws. She was going to grow into a huge dog, he guessed.

'No, I don't think ...' he started, then heard a commotion behind him.

He turned around to see Luda, Michael and Anya all nodding their heads. 'Dad, *please*,' Anya said, her eyes shining. He looked at Luda and she grinned. He was so happy to see that, he didn't hesitate.

'Well, I think the decision's already made,' he said. 'Yes, we'll have her.'

Anya immediately named her Molly, and Molly quickly became an important member of the family. Nick imagined that at some point along the line, her ancestors had been bred to hunt kangaroos – with the speed of the Great Dane, the jaw of the mastiff and the

Labrador's obedience and appetite. Molly, however, must have been a great disappointment to her dam and sire. Although she grew quickly, and possessed the loudest bark, she turned out to be scared of everything, and especially kangaroos. 'She was the biggest wuss going,' says Nick. 'But we all fell in love with her.'

Molly proved a great distraction too from Nick and Luda's mounting worries, with news at that point filtering through of the sudden and mysterious death, just outside London, of one of Putin's most vocal critics. Oligarch and politician Boris Berezovsky, an outspoken opponent of the President, had been granted political asylum in Britain in 2003, after which constant attempts by Russia to extradite him had failed. In 2012, Berezovsky had brought an ultimately unsuccessful high court action against Chelsea Football Club owner Roman Abramovich over the ownership of a major oil company. But in March 2013 Berezovsky had been found dead in his home and a coroner had just recorded an open verdict. The reports sent a chill down Nick's spine. Some commentators used his death to suggest that enemies of Putin were as unsafe in Britain as they were in Russia. It added an extra urgency to Nick's entreaties.

The earliest Nick could submit his latest Ministerial Intervention application was July 2013, by which time Rudd was back as Prime Minister, with Tony Burke in the immigration role, albeit with a changed title, the Minister for Immigration, Multicultural Affairs and Citizenship. By now, Nick had discovered the new complementary protection grounds but, every time he brought it up with a departmental officer, he was told he wasn't a suitable candidate. 'Without a lawyer to argue the case, I didn't seem to have a chance,' Nick says. 'So, in the end, I thought they must be right and didn't pursue it further. If only I'd have known . . .'

Shortly afterwards, on 7 September 2013, the Coalition stormed back into power on a platform of Operation Sovereign Borders – a military-style response to 'stopping the boats' and clamping down on illegal migrants. By 18 September, the department had been renamed Immigration and Border Protection.

None of these developments seemed to bode well for the Stride family. Predictably and in due course, their application for Ministerial Intervention was again denied. This time it was by the new Immigration Minister Scott Morrison, working under Prime Minister Tony Abbott.

Russia was back in the news, as well, with its invasion and annexation of the Crimean Peninsula from Ukraine in February 2014 following the Maidan Revolution against the pro-Russian government. Many international observers warned that this could lead to an escalation in hostilities between the two countries.

Nick read about it all gloomily, and then asked for a meeting with the British Consulate in Perth. He wanted to ask if his family could return as a unit to the UK, rather than have Luda sent back to Russia, which now seemed determined to flex its muscles on the world stage. It wouldn't be the ideal solution, he knew that, and they could well spend the rest of their lives looking over their shoulders, but it seemed the only way they'd be able to stay together.

A meeting was arranged but the result was poor. The head of the British Consulate said Luda had no rights to enter the UK, even as the spouse of a UK citizen, unless she met certain strict criteria. On the basis of her immigration record in the UK, however, having previously overstayed her visa to give birth to Anya, he said that would be highly unlikely. Nick was taken aback. He'd expected a meeting at which he could present all the information about his family and this would be taken away to be considered at length. Still, the British official did provide his email address, and Nick emailed him the next day asking for a meeting with consulate staff to make an application for Luda. There was no response.

Nick made one last-ditch attempt for Ministerial Intervention, filling in yet more forms and submitting them to Morrison and his then Assistant Minister Michaelia Cash. Neither was renowned for being sympathetic towards asylum seekers, but there was no other option. Nick also contacted his local federal Member for Forrest, Nola Marino, who agreed to a meeting and was sympathetic, promising to contact Cash on Nick's behalf. But despite several follow-ups by Nick, nothing happened. He then appealed to the Western Australia Department of Child Protection and Family Support, saying that someone was threatening to remove Luda from her children. They seemed concerned . . . until they found out the 'someone' was the department.

Nick, at that point, confided in their friend, the police officer Steve Delane, what was happening. 'I think it took Nick a bit of time to feel like he could trust us,' Delane says. 'He'd mentioned that they were trying to get residency but now I could see how much they were struggling with it all. It felt like a really heartbreaking story. Nick had certainly had an adventurous life and was resilient and resourceful, but I could see he wanted a home for his family somewhere and yet he was coming up against all this red tape and a system that didn't work very well.

'You could get through if you had enough money or the right connections, but if you had neither, it could be pretty tough. They wanted to put you into particular boxes and if you didn't quite fit into any of them, it looked impossible. I could see the turmoil he was in at the prospect of his family being torn apart. It disgusted me to see how badly the system worked. It wasn't as if they only had to go to Perth every six months, either. It was every fortnight and sometimes even weekly. Here was a family who might not have fitted into a particular compartment, but they certainly did deserve consideration on compassionate grounds. They were good people and wanted to fit in and contribute and help others. It frustrated me and made me angry.'

Nick tried to block it all from his mind, but it was proving impossible. Not six weeks later, newspapers, radio and TV were again filled with images of Putin after a Malaysian Airlines flight, MH17, en route from Amsterdam to Kuala Lumpur, crashed and burned in eastern Ukraine on 17 July 2014, killing all 298 people on board, thirty-eight of them Australians. It had been flying over an area where Russian-backed separatists and government forces were fighting, and immediately afterwards, Ukraine produced intercepted audio transmissions which it claimed were evidence that the separatists had shot down the plane. The world was outraged and demanded answers, and Australia went into mourning.

In the meantime, Nick had finally made contact with the journalist Michael Weiss in New York, but the writer was cautious about trusting Nick. He asked him to send over a couple of his documents so he could verify them and assess whether Nick would be a reliable source. Nick did so and Weiss immediately came back for more. He was so concerned about keeping the next stage of his investigation confidential, he insisted that all correspondence between the pair be via sophisticated encryption services; phone, emails, texts and Skype were just too vulnerable to hackers. They talked, and Nick sent more documents, relieved to have something to distract him from the corrosive anxiety of their situation.

He was interested that Weiss was so keen on writing about Shuvalov and started to research the latest information about his old boss. After Putin had become president again, it seemed Shuvalov had remained in his post as the first deputy prime minister, now to the former president and new Prime Minister Medvedev. He was still very much a rising star of the Russian regime and responsible for the federal budget and economic policies. But as Nick read more, he realised Shuvalov was beginning to face difficulties at home.

These seemed to have started in December 2011 when the American weekly magazine-newspaper *Barron's*, published by Dow Jones & Company, had reported on Shuvalov's business dealings with a tycoon and then on questions about his alleged role in granting government loan guarantees to that man's company.

Three months later, on 28 March 2012, a *Wall Street Journal* investigation published allegations that Shuvalov, whom it called 'one of Vladimir Putin's closest lieutenants', had, over the past twelve years, an offshore account that had earned tens of millions of US dollars investing with some of Russia's most powerful tycoons. It said that, according to financial records and people familiar with his investments, his holdings included a stake in the gas giant OAO Gazprom and an option on shares in a major oil company, and that he'd reported income more than ten times that of most of the other cabinet members. It added, however, that there was no indication the transactions violated Russian laws and quoted Shuvalov saying, 'I've unswervingly followed the rules and principles of conflict of interest. For a lawyer, that's sacred.' A spokesperson for Putin said Shuvalov regularly informed him about his financial dealings.

Yet the heat showed little sign of letting up. Russian *Forbes* magazine had written a massive feature on Shuvalov on 3 May the same year, claiming that, as first deputy prime minister, he had earned more than US$200 million based on public deals and found himself at the centre of a corruption scandal. It said he'd done business with many people involved in the *Forbes* Golden Hundred, including Abramovich, that some aspects of his transactions were 'scandalous' and that a meeting of the Anti-Corruption Council under President Putin was to be held, with 4000 people in just two days joining the closed Facebook community 'Shuvalov in the dock'. It alleged he formed a trust or a company registered in the Bahamas for his assets, put in the name of his wife Olga, and that, as a public servant, he was involved in various business activities that constituted a conflict of interest and made him, or his wife, a great deal of money. It also said he had several foreign cars in his car park, including a Jaguar and two Mercedes-Benz, had a number of apartments in Moscow as well as two large landholdings in the Moscow region, a huge apartment in London and a house in Austria. When confronted with the allegations by *Forbes*, Shuvalov was reported as either denying them or saying nothing.

Nick was transfixed. It seemed that Putin's golden boy was beginning to look a little tarnished. But there was one more recent newspaper report he read that filled him with dread. Shuvalov, it appeared, was about to visit Australia as Russia's chief representative at the G20 talks that were scheduled for Brisbane the next month, in mid-November. Nick could feel sweat form on his brow as he thought of being in the same country as Shuvalov. Even if there were thousands of kilometres between them, it still felt too close for comfort.

The world seemed to be closing in. Even when it was confirmed that Putin himself would be attending, instead of Shuvalov, despite a poll showing that forty-nine per cent of Australians didn't want to let him into the country because of the Crimean annexation and the shooting down of MH17, Nick still felt sick at heart. And by now, the tension at home was palpable.

'Mum and Dad tried to hide their worries from us, but it was impossible,' Michael says. 'Every day, every week, they'd be waiting for an email or a phone call from Immigration. I suppose I didn't really understand the significance of it, but I knew it was important. Dad was very stressed out every day.'

Anya, too, knew that something bad was going on. 'They were both very worried and distraught, but they tried to keep it hidden from us,' she says. 'They tried to protect us.'

The next important letter came on 29 October 2014: Morrison and Cash had vetoed their final request for intervention.

ANU Russian academic Dr Leonid Petrov has great sympathy for Nick and his family. He says, back then, a lot of countries had no idea of the potential threat Russia could pose. 'The understanding of Putin's regime was very different in the second decade of the 21st century to what it is now,' he says. 'The events of 2022 and the war with Ukraine showed they are capable of creating a lot of trouble long-term, all the way to the possibility of using nuclear weapons, and also demonstrated how little regard they have for human rights or UN conventions. If Nick and his family had applied for refugee status now in Australia after threats made by Russians, they might have had a significantly different outcome.'

But in late 2014, with their final rebuff, the heat was turned up to roasting point. Nick and Luda went back into the department but staff said there were no more appeals left and there was now only one option, the familiar one: Nick and the children would have to go back to the UK, while Luda would be sent back to Russia.

This time, Nick couldn't stop the tears flowing down his own face as Luda – his strong, beautiful Luda – again wept silently beside him. 'Please,' he begged, '*please* don't do this. We'll do anything to be allowed to stay. You'll be sentencing us all to death. We just want to be together. Is that too much to ask?'

Apparently, it was. The officers remained impassive. 'It's the rules,' they said, over and over. 'There's nothing else we can do. If you do not leave of your own volition, we will put your wife on a plane to Russia ourselves, and you and your children on a plane to Britain. You have three weeks to leave the country.'

# FOURTEEN
# THE CHOICE

THAT AFTERNOON, WITH THE kids still safely at school, Nick and Luda drove down to Bunbury's Back Beach, a place the whole family had come to love for its golden sands and crystal-clear water. This time, they parked but made no move to get out of the car and walk down the steps from the road over the dunes to the shoreline. Instead, they stayed inside, wound up the windows and then both screamed and screamed at the top of their voices until finally collapsing in each other's arms, sobbing as if their hearts would break.

The couple sat like that for an hour before Luda pulled away and turned a tear-stained face to Nick. 'Promise me you won't leave me,' she begged. 'Promise me you won't take the children away.' Nick nodded silently. He couldn't trust himself to speak.

They drove back to their little house and made coffee and waited for the children to arrive home. Nick checked his emails and found one from Michael Weiss. He rubbed his eyes as he read, hardly able to believe either its timing or what it contained. Weiss said he wanted to thank Nick for all the invaluable information he'd supplied and said the story he'd written about Shuvalov, using many of his documents as sources, was going to create a massive stir internationally. It would appear in the US news publication *Foreign Policy*, the specialty global affairs, current events and domestic and international policy news magazine, published by The FP Group, a division of the company that had formerly been The Washington Post Company. With the time difference between Australia and the US, it would come out in Perth on 29 October 2014, twelve hours after its appearance in New York, under the headline, 'The Kremlin's $220 Million Man'. And he quoted the write-off: 'Igor Shuvalov, Russia's deputy prime minister, is supposed to have the cleanest hands in the Kremlin. So where'd he get a quarter of a billion dollars?'

Nick blanched as he read the screen. He'd had no idea what many of the documents about Shuvalov on his hard drive had contained and didn't want to know. He'd never made any allegations about his old boss, but here was a famous and well-respected journalist writing a no-holds-barred exposé, loaded with allegations which, if true, would be damning. Nick silently thanked God that Weiss hadn't named any of his sources.

As he went through the article, he could feel his hair stand to attention. Weiss wrote that the winter gardens project Nick had been working on had grown from the original plan of a modest kind of retreat to a 'Gatsby-style' estate that was now costing a stunning US$140 million. He alleged Shuvalov was avoiding customs tax by using other banks and offshore schemes to mask transactions, and other people, like his former chauffeur and his multi-millionairess wife Olga, as names to run certain companies. Even so, Weiss said, he was currently the highest-earning government official in Russia,

Anya plays with her favourite pig, Long Legs, at Banana Well, with the chickens joining the melee. But even her fondest pet ends up, by necessity, on the barbecue.

Anya, 14, with a Stimson's python, one of the many pet snakes she keeps at Banana Well for company.

The wet season build-up at Banana Well is always menacing, but when the rains break, it's usually even worse, smashing everything in their path.

Michael, 16, helps the Nyul-Nyul rangers trap and catch a dangerous croc that's been menacing the local community.

At Pender Bay, three hours north of Banana Well, the family takes the Burrguk community ute to visit local families on the peninsula.

That old ute becomes their lifeline, a way of getting to Broome to pick up supplies once a month.

Storms hit with incredible ferocity on the Dampier Peninsula and often lightning strikes ignite raging fires.

Arriving at the family's next stop, Red Shells, in June 2017, with the old HiLux again proving the most reliable bush basher of them all.

July 2017 and now at their final stop on the peninsula, a place so lonely it doesn't even have a name until they nickname it 'The Beach'. Bush mechanic Michael, 17, is forever doing running repairs to keep the HiLux on the road.

Michael takes a rest at their camp in the heat at The Beach.

Luda makes a sparse dinner of rice and fish over a campfire at The Beach.

August 2018 and Anya, 17, and Michael, 18, say a fond farewell before Michael leaves for Vietnam to try to renew his visa, having no idea they'll be separated for so long.

Michael helps an elderly street seller carry her wares in Saigon, as he battles to make friends on his own.

Together again at last. July 2023 and Nick, 55, Michael, 23, and Anya, 22, finally make a new home, having been granted asylum in New Zealand – but all are still longing to return to Australia.

making US$6.3 million the previous year, only slightly more than his wife's US$6.2 million over the same twelve months.

In an earlier interview that year, Shuvalov had answered other critics, saying he hadn't done anything wrong, and fully complied with Russian law, with foreign assets held in a kind of blind trust. He said he'd made his fortune when working in private enterprise.

But as Nick read on, a wave of despair swept over him. This couldn't have come at a worse time. 'I hadn't made any allegations against Shuvalov myself, but I'd given information to a third party that had been used to allege that he was corrupt,' Nick says. 'And it was coming out just as Shuvalov was preparing to visit Brisbane for the G20 Summit that was due to start in two weeks' time. With Russian money invested throughout the world, you'd expect some oligarchs to have money in, and dealings with, companies in Australia too. If we'd just *suspected* we'd be in trouble with the Russians up to that point, now we definitely knew we could be in serious danger.'

Associate Professor Matthew Sussex says Nick was right. 'Releasing information like he did would almost always lead to some form of retaliation,' he says. 'And when it comes to documents that might reveal otherwise hidden information, that's not something that tends to go unpunished. Government elites can be particularly sensitive, as well as the organised criminal cabals who float around.'

Ironically, that whistleblowing could have given Nick and his family an even stronger case to be granted asylum, with an argument to be made that whistleblowing should fall under one of the five grounds of the convention – political opinion. Maria O'Sullivan, an Associate Professor in the Deakin Law School in Melbourne, who regularly comments on human rights and refugee issues, says that, although she hasn't read the tribunal's decision, Nick and his family might have been hard done by.

'I believe that he would have had a good case to link the retaliation he was facing to the Refugee Convention ground of political opinion, she says. 'I am therefore not sure why his refugee case was rejected . . . perhaps because the tribunal member did not think whistleblowing was an act of political opinion. There is not much legal authority on this.'

But totally unaware of this other possibility, Luda just couldn't stop sobbing, and Nick was sorely tempted to join her. But instead, he tried to stay calm. He emailed Weiss back and explained their situation, that Luda was at risk of being sent back to Russia and he and the kids banished to Britain. Weiss was appalled and immediately offered to write a letter to Morrison to add his considerable weight to Nick's campaign to be allowed to stay. He was true to his word, but Morrison never replied.

Nick and Luda waited in silence for their children to return home. Michael, now fourteen and a handsome, well-built boy, came in first, and Nick gestured to him to come with him. They went outside, and Nick drove again to Back Beach, and they sat together in the car, overlooking the ocean. The family had always made decisions together and Nick was adamant that the children should be heard on this, perhaps the most important choice they'd all ever have to make.

Nick did his best to explain the situation to his son. 'Basically, they're refusing to let us stay here,' he told him. 'They're saying they're going to send Mum to Russia, and we have to go to Britain.'

Michael looked at him wide-eyed. 'They can't do that, can they?' he asked. 'That would be awful. What would happen to Mum over in Russia? Why can't she come with us?'

Nick shook his head in despair. 'Look, Michael, we've basically got two options,' he said, trying to keep his voice from breaking. 'Either we can let Mum go and we can go to England or . . . or . . .'

'What?' Michael asked.

'We can go on the run together. It won't be easy, but at least we'd still be together as a family. I want to know what you think. Would you rather say goodbye to Mum and then go over to England and live a normal life – without her – or would you rather go into the outback where we could all disappear together?'

Nick studied his son carefully. He says now that he felt it was critical that Michael had an equal say on choosing a path, as it would have a huge impact on his life. He was doing so well at school, with his NAPLAN scores, covering grammar, punctuation and numeracy, among the highest in Western Australia, and in the top band in all Australia, as well as in all his other pursuits, and he had a right to be heard. 'He was free to say no, that he didn't want to abandon his life to go out into the outback, and we would have taken that into account,' Nick says. 'We were making him a part of the whole process.'

Michael was silent for a moment, thinking about what his father had told him. 'So, I'd have to leave my school, my friends and my life here really?' he asked.

Nick put his arm around his son. 'Yes, mate, that's right.'

'But Mum could come with us if we did that?'

Nick nodded. He was so full of emotion he didn't dare speak. He realised he was holding his breath.

Michael frowned. 'I think we should stay as a family,' he said. 'We should try to disappear.'

Nick hugged his son hard. It was exactly what he hoped he might say.

Today, Michael says he realised at the time it was one of the most important decisions he'd ever be asked to make. 'Dad gave me the ultimatum – either go back to the UK and possibly never see Mum again, or we hide away in the outback. He explained the consequences of both choices. Disappearing into the outback would be tough, he said, but I thought never seeing Mum again would be tougher.

'We'd always moved around a lot, from England to Russia, to England again, then Australia, and while we were in Australia, we were moving a lot of the time, so it was almost as if we'd been practising all our lives for this. But it was hard. We were getting settled and integrating into Australian society and adapting to the Australian way of life. School was going well, work was good for my parents and we all had friends. But it felt as though this was something that had to be done. In my mind, it was a minor setback and we'd only be gone for, say, six months.'

Nick drove Michael back and the pair entered the house to find Luda again in tears, and Anya hovering near her looking worried. Nick gestured to Anya to follow him outside, where he tried to explain the situation to her, and ask what she thought.

She was only thirteen, and a quiet, shy girl, with long brown hair and a slow, thoughtful way of speaking. He'd always tried to protect her from what was happening around them but knew he could no longer hide the truth. 'The immigration authorities want us to go, and we might be in danger from other people who are after us,' he said.

Anya looked back at him, puzzled. 'Are we famous?' she asked. 'I didn't realise that we were famous.'

Despite himself, he couldn't help bursting into laughter. 'No, no, we're not,' he said. 'But we're certainly not popular with a lot of people.'

Anya remembers being too young to understand properly what was happening. 'I knew we were leaving because people were trying to send us to different countries,' she says now. 'I remember going to school and mentioning it to one of my friends, but my brother told me that maybe I shouldn't. So, then I kept quiet. But I said goodbye to a couple of friends and we gave away our goldfish and Chilli the parrot, which made me very sad, and we started packing up everything.

'I think I knew that at some point we would have to leave but I think I was lying to myself, and telling myself it would be a kind of holiday and it wouldn't be for long. But I knew in my heart that this could well be us leaving for good, but I just didn't want to really believe it. I was sad to leave but also just a little bit excited. I'd grown up having adventures with my family and I believed this could be the next one.'

But on the day her dad had taken her aside, they returned to the house and immediately Luda looked up at Nick to try to discern the expression on his face. He saw the anguish in her eyes, and his heart went out to her. 'Yep, the kids are set,' he reassured her. 'We're going to go on the run, to run for our lives.'

It was only the second smile he'd seen on her face in months.

Their friend Steve Delane suspected something was up. He'd listened as Nick made plans, then back-up plans, then back-ups for those back-ups. 'He always had half-a-dozen irons in the fire at any one time,' he says. 'It wasn't a surprise to find out they were thinking of heading off as I knew Nick and Michael liked camping and fishing and they were by now feeling like they had to do something and needed to disappear. My wife and I said we'd be happy to look after the kids so they could continue going to school, but Nick desperately wanted to keep them all together, and I understood that.

'My role as a WA police officer was about service and protecting others and I had a bit of an understanding of the system they were up against. So, their visa status wasn't a concern of mine. I just knew them as a lovely family who were honest and nice and willing to do things for other people. Nick was hard-working and he and Luda were doing some amazing stuff with their renovation business. The whole family were wanting to make a go of things and create a new life for themselves.'

Nick went around the house lighting candles as the electricity switchboard had been broken for weeks and they couldn't afford to get it fixed. Instead, they were having to get through the evenings in candlelight, although they charged their phones and laptops via the car battery. Then Nick's phone rang. It was Weiss. His voice was solemn. 'Nick, I'm sorry, but it's time to get yourself out of wherever you are to somewhere where people won't be able to find you,' he said quietly. 'We don't know what kind of reaction the Shuvalov camp might have over this, and you and your family could be in a lot of danger. So, now is the time to get yourself lost.'

Nick and Luda were suddenly spurred into action. They had no time to waste. And really, they had no choice about the path forward. They told the kids to pack their clothes and a few favourite possessions as they'd leave first thing in the morning. Then, they sorted out what camping gear they had from the last time they travelled around Australia and started packing it, took out all the cans they had in the pantry and went to the shops to pick up more food supplies and then loaded it all into their Nissan Patrol 4WD and the big two-wheel trailer it towed. It was then that the enormity of going on the run struck Anya.

'It all just hit me at once and I suddenly broke down and started begging Mum and Dad to stay just one more day so I could say a proper goodbye to all my friends,' Anya says. 'But they said it wasn't possible and we had to go right away. I was upset for a long time after that.'

Nick had enough worries for them all. 'We were absolutely panicking,' he says. 'That was it, we knew we had to go. We'd been warned we might be in danger from the Russians and the Australians didn't want us and wouldn't let us stay. But it was terrifying. Every time someone walked past the front door, we'd all stop and fall silent. We just didn't know who might turn up at our door. It might be Russians wanting to talk to us, or department officers coming to deport us. We had a Facebook page for work with our address on it; anyone who wanted to could have found us in five minutes. So, we knew we had to hurry.

'It's strange but I felt we'd been in danger before from the Russians, but it wasn't until Weiss published his article that the tide dramatically turned. At that moment, the danger suddenly became real. Very, very real.'

# PART THREE
# RUN FOR YOUR LIFE!

# FIFTEEN
# RUN FOR YOUR LIFE!

**BY THE TIME THE** sun rose at 5.20am on 30 October 2014, the little family were already well on their way towards an unknown destination in an uncertain future. They'd set out in the pitch black with Nick driving and Luda in the front seat beside him, and Michael and Anya in the back, with Molly curled up between them.

They were each lost in their own thoughts. Anya was thinking about the friends she was leaving behind in Bunbury and her school and their cosy little house. She wasn't sure where they were going or how long it would take them to get there, and she felt sad and lonely. This didn't feel anything like the last road trip they'd done around Australia which had been hugely exciting and the start of such a big adventure. This, by contrast, felt strangely dismal and ominous. She put her headphones on and turned on the little MP3 player her dad had bought her. Instantly, R.E.M.'s song 'Everybody Hurts' filled her ears.

'The lyrics just hit me, and I couldn't help tears running down my face,' Anya says. 'I don't know why, but I just felt so sad. Then I remember my dad kind of reaching behind his seat and holding my hand. I never thought about it at the time, but looking back, I think he was crying as well.

'So, I held his hand and looked out of the window, up at the stars. Something about them sort of comforted me. From that day on, every time I got upset – which was a lot – I would look up at the stars and try to feel better. But however hard I tried, it feels, from that moment on, that it all went downhill.'

Michael was also feeling glum. He'd tried to look cheerful for Anya but now, in the darkness of the car, he allowed himself to meander in his own headspace, trying to make sense of what was happening. He hadn't told any of his schoolfriends that he was leaving as he didn't want to attract too much attention. 'But I'm sure that all those people at school who thought I was a spy and called me a sleeper-cell agent would have thought us disappearing one night confirmed all their suspicions,' he says.

One of the things he'd packed to bring with him was his naval uniform, just in case they came back some day and he'd be able to resume his association with the sea cadets. He couldn't bear to leave that reminder behind, along with his blue bear and Russian cat, now also travelling with him for sentimental reasons. 'You know, when I was given the choice of what to do, it was picking between a bad option and an even worse option,' he says. 'I wanted a third option, which would have been, Can we have a visa, please? The immigration team in Perth might as well have been deporting an Australian because, at that point, I called myself an Australian, I wasn't anything else. I was in the Sea Cadets and wanted to serve Australia in the armed forces – how much more Australian can you get?

'I suppose I didn't fully appreciate what it meant to go and hide in the bush. I assumed we would be camping, but I didn't realise it would be survival camping, which is something else entirely. It was a really dark period. It felt like the tide had completely turned against us. And I think Dad felt ashamed that he couldn't protect us better, that he couldn't get the visa, that we'd had no power in the house, that we'd left all our stuff in a rental house for the owners to deal with when they'd done us a favour by charging us less rent, that we had so little money and food. But he had done his best. He always did his best by us.'

Nick was feeling morose, too. He'd taken a few moments to say goodbye to good friends in Bunbury and they'd been so upset, it had really distressed him. The doctor who'd examined Luda and written to the department in support was one of the toughest women Nick had ever met. Seeing her cry when he broke the news of their imminent departure was devastating. 'It was terrible that we'd broken her down, when she was so strong,' he says. 'I just hated our situation hurting other people and that's what it was doing.'

Delane had offered him advice about how to act if the family encountered any police while they were on the run. 'He'd said be nice, be polite, don't mention immigration, and say that there's nothing wrong, there's nothing to see here,' Nick says. 'He told me the police are actually not allowed to check our passports or visas unless they think there's something wrong, so don't give them any reason to think there's something amiss. And just say you're on holiday for two weeks here. The police won't really care. They have enough on their plate without picking up four fugitives and their dog.'

Nick smiled to himself at the thought of Molly. He could see her in the rear-view mirror snuggled up with the kids. She was proving a great addition to the family. He knew Anya had found it difficult leaving all her friends in Bunbury but at least she had Molly. She had a real gift with animals, Nick could see, and Molly was responding so brilliantly to her training, the family had come up with the nickname, 'The Dog Whisperer'. Molly, although she was fast becoming a big dog, fitted in perfectly with them all. After all, she hadn't been wanted either; another outcast.

Much later, Nick applied for his files from the department under the Freedom of Information (FOI) Act. One file chilled him to the core. It said that, at that point, *'status resolution officers have commenced removal planning. If Ms K and Mr Stride refuse to cooperate, status resolution officers will locate and detain them in an alternative place in detention as minor children are involved, and remove them in accordance with detention policy, ensuring the period of detention is as short as possible. Ms K would be removed to the Russian Federation, and Mr Stride, Michael and Anya would be removed to the UK.'*

They'd left in the nick of time, starting out that early morning with no clear idea of where to go, just the idea of heading north until they found a good place to hide out. The Kimberley in Australia's northwest, they knew from their first trip around Australia, was an exceptionally remote area, so that could be a possibility. They decided to keep one phone between them for emergencies, but agreed they wouldn't contact anyone they knew; they were only too aware that aiding a fugitive could be treated as an offence, and they didn't want to get anyone else into trouble. Of even more immediate concern, however, was their financial situation. They had only about $5000 to their name.

'That was a very limited amount of money we'd have to stretch out as long as we reasonably could,' says Nick. 'I knew there was going to come a time when it was all going to end, and probably badly. But we really didn't have a choice. I'd lost my first two children, and I couldn't sit by and see Luda lose hers. I thought the best thing would be if we kind of got lost for a while, and then just see what happened. And maybe things would change. Or maybe they wouldn't. But at least we were together. Anya once said that she thought our family motto should be, "We always find a way". She's right. I always think as long as you maintain a positive mind frame, then you can contribute to something positive happening. If you're negative, then there's only one outcome, and that's guaranteed to be bad.'

They drove quickly up through Fremantle and then through Perth, hardly daring to look out of the window in case they'd be spotted by someone who knew them from immigration or the police. Luda had never driven, so Nick was at the wheel constantly, heading up the Brand Highway until it hit the coast at the little port town of Dongara. There, they stopped to stretch their legs and Luda fed him and the kids brown-sauce sandwiches. Then they continued through Geraldton, with its rugged scenery and harrowing history of Dutch ships, like the *Batavia* and the *Zeewijk*, running aground on the rocky islands off the shoreline on their way up to Indonesia, with many of the survivors murdered. Nick shuddered to think of it. It matched his mood. They passed by the Kalbarri National Park, headed inland, then came back out again towards the coast at Carnarvon, on the mouth of the Gascoyne River. As the blackness of night fell, Nick pulled off the main road and, exhausted, slept where he sat. The others also slept inside the car, with the back open for air, too tired after their first day's fourteen-hour drive to attempt to put up one of their two pop-up tents.

From this point on, the Coral Coast became wild and wind-swept with few signs of life. Nick drove more carefully, knowing that any slip could mean the premature end of their expedition. He was growing tired, and everyone was becoming quieter, and he felt it was important to have a break and regroup. He considered stopping at Coral Bay, the little town on the way to Exmouth they'd all loved so much the time they'd driven down the coast, but then dismissed the thought. There would be too many tourists there visiting the Ningaloo Marine Park, too much curiosity and too many memories of happier, more optimistic days.

Instead, he decided they'd stop at Port Hedland, the largest town in Western Australia's Pilbara region, which the resources boom had turned into the world's biggest iron-ore port. Although he'd heard it was busy, noisy, dirty and pretty unpleasant, he also knew there were so many blow-ins and so many fly-in-fly-out workers, a little group of strangers wouldn't command any attention at all. They drove through the town to the local caravan park and this time set up the two tents, one for Michael to sleep in, and the other for Anya. Nick and Luda slept in the car. It was a relief not to be constantly moving and the family agreed they'd spend a second night there too for a break. Nick had noticed Anya was becoming tearful again as she'd been receiving messages from her friends on the family's phone and the realisation of what she'd left behind was beginning to sink in.

That morning, he suggested he and Anya take Molly for a walk to the bakery to buy some bread for breakfast, and he gently asked his daughter how she was feeling. She confessed that she was now having second thoughts about leaving Bunbury, and that maybe sticking with Mum hadn't been such a good idea. Nick reasoned with her and told her that soon they'd be at a nice beach where they'd be able to camp, and gradually everything would start to come together. He had no idea if it would, of course, but he felt a desperate need to reassure his youngest child. By the time they got back to the caravan park, she seemed appreciably happier.

'I think when we were driving, we were all quiet,' she says. 'We were all wondering what was happening, and where we were going, and when we'd get there. But it was better after we'd had a rest. I was teaching Molly a new trick and she was such a smart dog, she picked it up quickly. But she wasn't that smart that she knew to come back when there was another dog or a feral donkey or a dingo or anything wild that moved.'

The town was depressing with its hordes of orange hi-vis-jacketed workers, its red dusty streets, its higgledy-piggledy selection of shops, takeaway places, uninspiring cafes and the visitors centre. Most of the nice old buildings had been long blown away by cyclones, swept off by tidal surges, burnt down, eaten by white ants or bull-dozed. But it was a useful introduction to the dangers of outback Australia – with signboards warning of the local species of snakes: the desert death adder, the orange-naped snake, the common mulga or king brown, and the western brown snake.

They were all relieved when it came time to leave, and head off ever-northwards towards Broome in the Kimberley. It was a seven-hour drive on one of the most monotonous stretches of the Great Northern Highway, on the edge of Australia's second-largest desert, the unimaginatively named Great Sandy Desert, and they noticed how it seemed to be growing hotter and hotter with each passing kilometre. They had a break halfway at the Sandfire Roadhouse, quite possibly the most remote roadhouse in the country, and clambered out of the car to stand and stare at the vast, flat ochre dust plains that stretched out as far as the eye could see in every direction. If they were looking for a place to lose themselves, they were getting very close. Back on the road again, they all cheered when the odometer clicked up that they'd now driven 2000 kilometres north of Perth.

By the time they finally arrived in Broome early in the evening of 4 November 2014, it was wonderful to see the sea so close at hand, although it was uncomfortably hot at 39 degrees in the mid-afternoon, as well as horribly humid, and Nick could feel his shirt soaked in sweat the moment he got out of the car at the caravan park for their last night in civilisation. After this, Nick warned them, they would be free-camping on beaches with no drinking water, shower blocks, proper toilets, electricity or rubbish bins. His plan was for them to head off into the wild Dampier Peninsula, also known as Cape Leveque, where they mightn't see people for days, or weeks, at a time, he said. He could see Luda, Michael and Anya all looked nervous at the prospect, but he tried to cheer them up.

'It's going to be another great adventure,' he declared with an excitement he didn't feel. 'It's going to be beautiful, and fun.'

He had a guide that listed all the camping spots in the north-west, and he'd seen a free-camping place mentioned at an isolated beach at Quandong Point, about 50 kilometres north of Broome along a rough, unformed road. That, he thought, would be a good place to start. They shopped for more supplies in Broome the next morning – mostly water and more tinned food and bags of rice, as they had no fridge for storing fresh food, which would keep for barely an hour in such ferocious heat. Then they set off again and, as they drove up and parked on the red dust, scattered with saltbush, and looked out at the ochre cliffs, rocky, sun-bleached beach and the sapphire-blue ocean beyond, they had to admit it was a pretty place. But, yes, it also felt a long, long way from anywhere.

Nick and Michael set up camp with the two tents positioned behind the car for shelter from the hot wind, while Luda unpacked the water from the back of the car and Anya took Molly off for a walk to explore their new home. Then they gathered firewood for a fire later.

That evening, when they all sat around the fire in their camping chairs and ate their beans and rice, spirits were high. 'We just sat there and told jokes and had a great laugh,' Nick says. 'It felt for the first time that we were free. We were free of the Russians and we were free of Australian immigration, and we were all feeling good. Nothing mattered anymore. We were together, and we were in such a remote place, no one would ever find us.'

Michael also loved that first night. 'We played this game where we would count the satellites and the first person to see a shooting star would win,' he says. 'And I remember sitting back in our chairs and staring straight up at millions of stars, with no other lights or pollution.

'It was very beautiful but even in the middle of it, I remember thinking, *What's happened to get us to this point? Why are we here? And what is the future going to hold?* I had no idea.'

# SIXTEEN
# ANOTHER WORLD

THAT FIRST NIGHT, neither Michael nor Anya slept well. They constantly heard strange shuffling noises outside their tents and both wondered what the hell was out there, perhaps trying to get in. When the sun rose and, bleary-eyed, they unzipped their tents, the mystery was solved. It had been thousands upon thousands of hermit crabs, attracted by the bread and HP sauce they'd left out after making sandwiches. They were all piled on top of each other, with some piles almost as big as coconuts.

'It was an amazing sight,' Michael says. 'They [the hermit crabs] were harmless. There were plenty of other things out there which were a lot more dangerous. After that, though, we were always careful to put our food away.'

They spent that day exploring their new home, pushing their way through vegetation to find paths, clambering over rocks, fishing from the bigger boulders and playing with Molly on the sand. They checked out tidal pools and spotted turtles and dozens of deadly blue-ringed octopus, then collected more firewood and cooked up another big pot of rice, which they had for lunch, with the rest kept for dinner. Nick organised a quiz for both kids, they watched a stunning sunset that turned the whole world an even more fiery red than the place was normally and, around the fire that night, their dad told them about his own youth, growing up in England.

'Dad is a great storyteller,' says Anya. 'He told us some fascinating stories and made us laugh. We also played a lot of games; he did everything he could to keep us occupied. But that night, a one-metre-long snake slithered under my chair. It made me jump, but it didn't scare me. I love snakes, and always have. Besides, it had already gone, so it was too late to worry. Things like that happen and you just deal with it.

'The worst thing for me were all the mosquitoes, millions of them, and all the insects. It was the start of the rainy season, so there were so many things biting us. I counted fifty bites on one leg one day. They were so itchy, too.'

The days began to merge into one. They caught a few fish, mostly rock cod and the odd small snapper to supplement their rice and beans. But life was hard work. They all missed having showers as it was so hard to keep clean, and it wasn't as if they could swim in the sea because of the ever-present threat of lurking crocodiles, those blue-ringed octopus and deadly stonefish ruled out that option. They'd wade in occasionally while fishing but were always wary of unwelcome company. When the tide went out, the rock pools left in the reef contained a treasury of little fish, clams and other shellfish, but they quickly learnt to be careful not to get caught out by the incoming water. It felt like another world entirely, where everyone had to live on their wits.

After a week, Nick and Luda sat down on the rocks to decide what they should do next. They were aware of how little money they had to sustain them in the long term, and already their supplies of food and water were running low. They discussed their situation and decided that maybe one of them should try to find work in Broome to keep the family going.

Six days later, Nick announced he'd go back into Broome to restock on water, beans and rice. Michael and Anya went with him and for all of them it was a shock being among so many people again, both locals and tourists. At the supermarket, Nick glanced at a newspaper, and was taken aback to see a photograph of Putin on the front page. It seemed that he had attended the G20 summit himself in Brisbane after all, and Nick couldn't resist buying a copy.

They'd missed a great deal while living off the grid. Russia had sent a fleet of warships to international waters off the Australian coast to accompany their president, and the host nation had responded by sending two of their ships, and a surveillance plane, to keep an eye on their visitors. Prime Minister Tony Abbott had threatened to 'shirtfront' Putin over the MH17 – 'brought down by Russian-backed rebels using Russian-supplied equipment', he'd said – but in the end did no such thing. Other world leaders had given Putin a chilly reception, the newspaper reported, but had won no reassurances from him about either Ukraine or MH17.

Nick sighed and dumped the paper into the nearest bin. He could do without reminding himself of what, and who, his family were hiding from. He loaded up the car with supplies and then stopped off at the little fishing shop in town to buy some bait. As he walked up to the doorway, a sign in the window caught his eye: Caretakers Wanted. He looked more closely. The owners of a little holiday place on the Dampier Peninsula, the Goombaragin Eco Retreat, were planning a trip to Brisbane for a couple of months and wanted someone to keep the place going in the wet season. Nick asked about it in the shop. The place was just two hours away to the north, the fishing-shop manager told him, and it was a nice spot with beautiful views of Pender Bay. He told Nick he should give it a go.

Nick phoned the names on the card, Kathleen and John. They sounded delighted to hear from him and asked how soon he could start. They just needed someone to be there to make sure the place was kept tidy since there were rarely any guests at that time of year, and to deter intruders. Moreover, the retreat had a deluxe cliff-top chalet, some cabins and tents, and they said the family could have a cabin. When Nick told the kids, Anya was thrilled. She'd secretly hated living in a tent on the beach, battling the mosquitoes every night, and often ended up crying herself, as quietly as she could, to sleep.

'I knew we were only staying there because it was free,' she says. 'I knew our money was running out. But I remember disliking it so much. I had a little thin foam mattress and when it rained it would get wet and I'd be lying there in a puddle. But I didn't want to complain or tell anyone how I felt. We didn't have much choice, and I didn't want Dad to feel any worse than he already did.'

They drove back to Quandong Point and broke the good news to Luda. She was delighted and the next day they packed up their camp and set off to Goombaragin, around 170 kilometres north of Broome. When they arrived, the couple greeted them warmly and showed them the resort, with its background of red pindan cliffs, wild woodlands and private coastal bays. Nick had been nervous

they might ask why they were there, and had been working out
what to say but, in the event, they didn't ask a single thing. 'I kind
of said we were just travelling around, but I soon found that no one
on the peninsula up there ever asks any questions. That's because,
nine times out of ten, people are up there for one reason and one
reason only: to escape from something.'

The retreat felt like the lap of luxury compared to where they'd
been living. A ten-hectare eco-resort, it operated on solar power
with a grey and black water recycling treatment plant and had an
open fireplace in the middle of the camp where, during the tourist
season, Kathleen and John would cook freshly caught seafood
for their guests. Aboriginal guides from the local communities
that dotted the region would also come in to talk to them about
country and culture and show them some of the special spots in
the area.

The couple cooked some crocodile out of their freezer to welcome
the family and also talked to Nick about how to cope through the
wet. Then John suggested Nick and Michael follow him in his car
as he had to drive to a shop at a nearby community for something
critical as a cyclone was on its way. They set off as the rain began
and, within minutes, the road was completely under water. John's
car slid off the road and Nick towed him back on, and John reluctantly agreed they should go back. It turned out the critical item
he was after had been cigarettes. But as soon as the couple left, the
major problem with the down season reared its head. Another kind
of visitor moved in: snakes.

'Goombaragin was our first real taste of the bush,' says Michael.
'There were snakes everywhere. At night, you could stand in any
spot and shine a torch and it was guaranteed you'd see them.

You learned pretty quickly to be careful where you walked and, if you picked something up off the ground, you always jumped back in case there was a snake under it. The young ones were the worst. The adult snakes would want to preserve their venom so might slither away, but the young snakes would move so quickly and couldn't control their venom, so if they felt under threat, they'd just inject you with everything they had. The other nuisance were the horseflies. They could be as big as your thumb and, when they bit, it was really painful.'

The family weren't being paid for being at the camp but were told they could eat anything from the well-stocked freezers in lieu of wages, and an Aboriginal woman living nearby showed Michael and Anya how to hunt for bushtucker and what to pick and when, pointing out berries that would be poisonous if the outside shell was broken. Another Indigenous family invited them over for a meal, which turned out to be curried turtle, a creature normally protected but which can be hunted legally by First Nations people. It would have been considered extremely rude to refuse. Similarly, the time they were served dugong by another couple. 'I imagine not many white people have ever eaten dugong,' Nick says. 'It was like a really rich pork and, I've got to say, delicious!'

If they needed anything else, the nearest store was at Ardyaloon, or One Arm Point, a 400-strong Aboriginal community about an hour's drive away at the tip of the peninsula, but as the rains set in, the dirt road became impassable. Under all the water, the massive ruts and dips in the road couldn't be seen and, after that day when John slid off the road, they realised how treacherous it might be to have an accident with no help anywhere around. One day, Anya even went swimming in a massive pool that formed on the track.

Other days, they'd watch the incredible lightning storms and driving rain, look out for humpback whales and manta rays, see the sea eagles swooping down on the tuna, and then sit around outside at night around the fire, during breaks in the rain, staring up at the stars.

'It was the best time as we were comfortable and we didn't have too many worries,' Nick says. 'I think we all felt like the Swiss Family Robinson. I'd received about 200 emails from the department but it all went silent the day we left. We received one email from them in December to wish us – bizarrely – a Happy Christmas. It was almost as if they were saying, Don't come back! You're a problem we don't want to deal with.'

That Christmas, the family picked a big branch up off the ground, took it to the unit and decorated it like a Christmas tree. 'That was good but at the same time, it was kind of sad,' Anya says. 'We'd never had a normal Christmas as we didn't have any money, and you think of other people celebrating.'

In the New Year, on 10 January 2015, Kathleen and John returned with good news. The community at Ardyaloon, they said, was looking for a volunteer. Nick was intrigued. The community had originally been established on Sunday Island off the coast in 1899 and had stayed until 1960 when the Uniting Church Mission, which had taken it over, was closed down. Everyone was relocated to either Broome or Derby but, as saltwater people who traditionally fished and hunted, they couldn't adapt to town life and had moved to Ardyaloon instead. Now they wanted someone to help them carry out repairs and maintenance to the community's houses. In return, they'd supply food and accommodation.

It proved a good deal for everyone. Nick and the family were given a small two-room office to sleep in and told they could have anything they wanted from the community store. In return, Nick and Michael refitted, refurbished and repainted the dilapidated dongas in which the elders lived, installed new electricity switches into others' homes, put in air conditioning units and replaced rotting doors and window frames. Otherwise, the community would have had to engage tradies from Broome, who'd charge a $700 fee just to drive up there to check what needed to be done.

'People were ecstatic that they had someone who knew how to do this work there,' Nick says. 'They were very friendly and grateful. That was another nice time. We all got on very well. I think we were popular there . . . apart from Molly. A lot of people were nervous around such a big dog.'

Michael didn't mind it, either. Although he missed Bunbury, his school and the Sea Cadets – he still snuck a look at his uniform from time to time – he learnt a huge amount about building and construction, although he was impatient to move on. 'But I realised it was something we had to do,' he says. In his downtime, he loved going down to the water with his dad and sister, where they'd often feed the sharks with fish heads left over from their meals. 'They were mostly nurse sharks and they'd swarm up and take the food almost out of your hand,' Michael says. 'Then the bull sharks would come too and you'd hear their jaws snap shut so loudly as they're so strong . . . That was incredible.'

Anya always managed to keep herself busy. She would climb a big tree by the unit every day to check on the bird's nest there, and then watch the chicks hatch and learn to fly. She also wandered the beaches with Luda, both looking for subjects to draw, and ended up sketching the scenery as well as turtles, shells, camp dogs, lizards and, always, more snakes. The area was well known for both crocodiles and sharks, and sometimes you could see up to fifty sharks at any one time close to the beach feeding on fish. Everyone still swam in the ocean there, however, or fished while wading in waist deep, although always watching out for killer sharks coming too close.

She also made friends with some of the local Aboriginal people and spent time with one boy, Max, who was a few years younger. He showed her how to catch snakes using pillowcases tied at one end and then handle them, although not always successfully. One day, she was sitting at the family's dining table handling a baby Stimson's Python to get it used to human contact when it nipped her sharply on the finger. In fright and shock, she flung it away across the table towards where Michael was sitting looking at his computer. He barely even noticed. Mostly, though, Anya and Max kept their snakes in tubs that they decorated with shells and rocks before studying them and releasing them a few days later.

'I was thirteen and had been feeling really lonely and confused by what we were doing,' Anya says. 'I still didn't understand. I think I was a bit too young to comprehend it, and I missed my friends from school, so it was nice to have a friend there. Me and Max also caught lizards as pets and kept a scorpion in a salad bowl that we used to feed with these huge black beetles with massive pincers. The scorpion and the beetles were about the same size, and I often wondered if they'd fight, but the beetles never survived. One of my snakes escaped one day somewhere in the unit and Mum was furious as she never liked snakes.'

By the time of Anya's fourteenth birthday in January 2015, the family had been just over two months on the run, but she was trying to stay positive. That day, Max and his mum took her and Luda to one of the beaches and showed them a secret cave, considered sacred by their people, that was filled with fossils, one of which was given to Anya as a gift.

'I think that was the best birthday I've ever had,' she says now. 'I thought that was very special. It rained when we got back and it was so beautiful. The rain up north is something you'll never forget. It's not rain like you find anywhere else. It was warm and it turned the ground an even deeper red and it just made everything come alive. Mum made me a cake from the supplies at the store, too.'

By mid-March, all the jobs that needed doing had been done, and Nick started to worry about where the family could hide out next. They all seemed to be holding up fairly well, although Nick was troubled that Anya often seemed quiet and withdrawn. He wondered, as he did most days, whether they should call this whole escapade off and go back to civilisation and just deal with the consequences. Maybe the immigration authorities would take pity on them, and the Russians would leave them be.

That night, he skimmed the news on his computer. The Australian Human Rights Commission had just released the results of its inquiry into the 800 children being held by the government in immigration detention and slammed it as a breach of their rights. Nick wondered if perhaps the mood was turning more in favour of migrants . . . until he saw Prime Minister Abbott had savaged the report and said he felt no guilt whatsoever about the detention of children.

He flicked over to check the latest news from Russia and Nick's shoulders slumped. Shuvalov was in the headlines. He'd spoken at the World Economic Forum in Switzerland, warning the west against trying to topple Putin and saying the Russians were ready to sacrifice everything for their leader and would never give him up. 'Never!' he was quoted as saying. 'We will survive any hardship in the country, eat less food, use less electricity.'

And then a smaller news item caught Nick's eye. This was about a Russian whose name was very familiar: Boris Nemtsov. He'd been a former deputy prime minister – the position Shuvalov was now holding – under Boris Yeltsin but had later become one of the fiercest and most outspoken critics of Putin. He'd spoken a few days before at a news conference in Moscow alleging corruption at the Winter Olympics held in Russia's Sochi in February 2014 and had also been helping to organise a rally to protest Russia's military intervention in Ukraine. As Nick read, the words on the screen started to blur.

Two days before that demonstration, Nemtsov had been walking home from a restaurant with his girlfriend when halted just metres from the Kremlin. He was shot four times in the back and died on the spot.

# SEVENTEEN

# CREATURES GREAT AND SMALL

THERE WAS NOW NO question in Nick's mind that they'd have to stay in hiding, but everyone was starting to get anxious about where they could disappear to next. Anya reminded them again, however, of their family motto: 'We always find a way.'

And, true to form, they did. An Aboriginal friend called around one morning to say that the Burrguk Aboriginal Community, about 140 kilometres north of Broome, was also looking for some outside help and would be happy to have the four of them come live with them.

Nick and Luda studied their map of the area. The Burrguk community, made up of the Nyul Nyul people, ran a bush campsite called the Banana Well Getaway on the Beagle Bay Creek. It had started out as a banana plantation and market garden, with goats and chickens, operated by one of the brothers of the Pallottine monks who'd operated a mission in the area. This brother had married a local Aboriginal woman and they'd barter and sell their produce, as well as fresh water from their well, to the pearling luggers.

In recent years, a number of accommodation blocks and a three-bedroom house had been built on the site, and camping grounds laid out.

The family drove down on 17 March 2015 to take a look. The getaway lay on the creek, a huge and hostile place of tidal black soil, mud, mangroves, sandflies and crocodiles. Banana Well was rudimentary but during the tourist season they had plenty of visitors coming to fish, bush-bash and get away from it all. Unlike Ardyaloon, there was no one else living there; the population was much more thinly scattered between Derby and Broome. The Strides' job would be to run the getaway, and for as long as they wanted to.

They decided to stay and that first night, sleeping in one of the units, they quickly realised why what looked like a dream care-taking job wasn't more popular. Throughout the night, they were constantly dive-bombed by countless mosquitoes. 'There were a lot of paperbark trees around a huge marshy area, and so whether you were walking around, sitting down or sleeping, you'd have a thick halo of mosquitoes around you,' Nick says. 'At first, we were religious about smothering ourselves with mosquito repellent and got through so many cans, but it didn't seem to make any difference. It wasn't long before we just gave up. I think we were all bitten so many times, we ended up impervious to them. But it seemed they were the reason that so many guests came and stayed just one night, then couldn't get away fast enough.'

Despite the mozzie curse, Nick could see there was a lot going for the place. There was a huge variety of birds, including egrets, brolgas and bee-eaters, lots of wallaroos, dingoes, wild donkeys and frilled-neck lizards, and the marshland was blooming with vivid wildflowers. There was also great boating and fishing to be had at the creek, with huge barramundi, giant trevally and lots of whiting, groper, cod, salmon and mud crabs to be caught, as well as crocodiles to be observed from a distance. Nearby was Beagle Bay itself with its beautiful Sacred Heart Church, famous Australia-wide for its stunning shell altar of mother of pearl, cowrie, volute and olive snail shells, built entirely by hand by local Aboriginal people and those Pallottine monks. That was another huge tourist draw.

Yet most visitors stayed that one night, and then decamped to one of the other, bigger and less mosquito-plagued campsites elsewhere on the peninsula. The books showed the site had made $56,000 the previous year, so Nick set out to see if he could improve on that. Every time one of the guests came in after their first night to say they were off, Nick would offer them a free crab net and bait for them to take down to the creek. If they didn't succeed in catching a crab, he'd promise them, they could stay another night on the house.

'But there were so many crabs down there, you'd guarantee they'd catch plenty and have such a good time that nine times out of ten, they'd stay another day,' he says. 'And then sometimes, another. And perhaps another. So, we managed to increase the average stay to three nights, and more than doubled the income. We also had a couple of houses there, one with three bedrooms and the other with four, so I came up with the idea of renting those out to the families of people working in Broome. I phoned up a lot of the companies there and said I had this accommodation and would provide food, and suddenly we had bookings for four months ahead, and for $400 a night.'

At that point, Nick realised that it would be hard to both hide and make a success of a tourist enterprise at the same time, so he took a deep breath, adopted the pseudonym of Nick Ashcroft, joined the Broome tourist association, talked to the local newspaper, the *Broome Advertiser,* about the campsite and advertised it as the first dog-friendly resort in the Kimberley. His efforts, bizarrely, even won him a tourism prize – a spa treatment in town that he never dared take up.

But the gamble had a price. Even though their time there was working out well, it was never stress-free. Every morning when Nick and Luda woke, they'd glance out to the gate at the entrance to the site to check they didn't have unwanted company, either someone from Australian immigration or someone, or a group, who might look Russian.

'Every single day, without fail, I'd look out and think, *Is this going to be the day when someone comes and destroys everything?*' Nick says. 'It might be hard for people to understand that, but it was hell. We tried to make the best of the circumstances, and we were making a success out of Banana Well and we did have some brilliant times, but always in the background there was real anxiety and depression. There wasn't a moment I wasn't thinking about what might go wrong.'

Michael was aware his dad was stressing every day about who might turn up, but he buckled down to help with the business. He helped Nick build more infrastructure around the place, like a pig pen, and took turns taking guests fishing.

Ironically, the police would regularly drop in, too. A female police officer arrived one day and said, 'Hi Nick. I'm just coming to check on you. Everything all right?'

Nick immediately suspected that the police had been briefed by the department and were keeping an eye on them. He had no proof and could never be sure, but the police visited so often, and were so assiduously casual and friendly, he couldn't help but believe they were part of a plot.

With the force having to cover the whole of the peninsula from their HQ at Lombadina, they often asked him for help, too – be it searching for missing people, locating fishermen who'd got lost in the salt marshes or mangroves, or pulling out cars that had got bogged in the marsh. The police there were equipped with large 4WDs but their insurance didn't allow them to drive off-road, so Nick would also attend any crashes that had happened on dirt roads, and bring the occupants back to his camp from where the police would pick them up. Another time, Broome Police phoned for 'Mr Ashcroft' and asked him to rescue two men who'd been sighted walking along a peninsula in states of visible distress. The only problem was, they had no idea where they were. Against all the odds, Nick and Michael eventually found them. They also tracked down a police officer who'd gone fishing and hadn't returned by nightfall and guided her back to safety.

'It could be such a treacherous place,' Nick says. 'We pulled rangers, police, Australian tourists and Chinese visitors out of the boggy marshes as they'd not realised how soft the mud was, or they'd gone too far in. There's a lot of water that bubbles up through the ground and it could appear in places where it wasn't the day before. Then there are the king tides that can make it even more dangerous. It was a very fast learning experience for us. One time, the rains came early and we had a puncture and had to change the tyre in three-foot-deep water, which was a nightmare trying to get the jack into. Another time, we were driving on the beach at Red Cliffs and we got bogged and the car was slipping down towards the rocks, but we immediately let down the tyres, propped the car up with more rocks and managed to get out. I think we started getting quite complacent that we could get ourselves out of anything.

'I remember once, during the build-up to the wet season, we had three of the Beagle Bay mob get stuck on the track and we got two vehicles stuck trying to get them out. In the end, I just took all their keys off them and told them to leave their cars there as we'd destroy the rest of the track before we got them out. I said I'd pull them out when it dried up and drop their keys back to them then. No one argued. We were always helping them out and we felt like valued members of the community.'

Yet there could be tricky local politics to navigate. One time, there was bad blood between the Burrguk Aboriginal community and the Beagle Bay mob, made worse by the excellent barramundi fishing at Banana Well. People from Beagle Bay, with a population of around 120, would often cross the campsite to get to the best fishing spots, so a crowd of Burrguk members drove up one day, dug a trench across the track they'd been using, knocked all the trees down around it to stop anyone getting through and then disappeared off back to Derby and Broome, leaving Nick to cope with the consequences. It was only a couple of hours later that an angry mob from Beagle Bay arrived to confront Nick and accuse him of trying to stop them fishing. Nick insisted instead that the track had been closed to stop white men from Broome coming up and stealing the fish . . . and, after an exceedingly tense stand-off, managed to convince them this was true. Only later was he told that the delegation had been sent up to 'beat the crap out of you'. But from that moment on, Nick was considered an ally by both sides.

Nature was a formidable enough foe on its own. Apart from the myriad dangerous creatures, every time anyone even brushed past a bush, they had to inspect their legs for tiny spikes. Also, because the landscape was so flat and dry outside of rainy season, fire was a constant threat. If the wind was blowing in the wrong direction, the flames could be threatening all and sundry even before they'd smelled the danger. Banana Well had a 2000-litre water tank for fighting fires, but it had so many holes in it, it was as good as useless. There were a few occasions when the family had to drape wet towels over their heads and try to stop an inferno spreading into their compound, beating the flying embers with shovels until their hands bled, while all around them it sounded as though a monster were approaching, with trees exploding in the heat.

'Fighting the fires was like a living hell,' says Michael. 'It was so dangerous as you knew any minute you could be swallowed up by the inferno. But we were desperate to protect our home and the buildings. It wasn't just the flames that were such a hazard, either. There was always the danger of heat stroke, and all the smoke inhalation could have proved deadly. We came close to losing so many times.'

The power and fury of the thunderstorms could be terrifying, too. One night, lightning hit the metal sheds with an almighty crash and Nick could see Luda's long hair standing on end. With lightning striking every half-second, he raced to Michael and Anya's unit to stop them touching anything metal and getting electrocuted. At that moment, a lightning bolt smashed into the Telstra tower and blew out all the electrics and the phone line. 'It was the loudest thing I've ever heard in my life,' Nick says.

Nick and Luda would troop into Broome maybe once a month for supplies. With no internet access at Banana Well – despite having that Telstra tower at their place, mobiles never worked for some reason so they relied on a landline and a satellite phone for emergencies – it was often a time to catch up on what was happening in the outside world. It was on one such visit that Nick discovered that Prime Minister Abbott had been deposed in a leadership contest by Malcolm Turnbull; meanwhile, Russia was cranking up its aggression, intervening in the civil war in Syria in September, and siding with the collapsing Assad regime against the US-backed Free Syria militias. Broome was also where the family gloomily huddled together to mark their first anniversary on the run on 30 October 2015, with a rare treat of takeaway burgers.

Back at camp, they made do the rest of the time with the blue-fin tuna, rock cod and mud crabs they caught, eggs from the ten chickens they kept, the wild cattle they shot for meat, and the feral donkeys they killed to feed Molly. They also kept pigs, ducks and guinea fowl.

'I went hunting a few times,' Michael says. 'It makes you really respect animal life when you do what you have to in order to survive. I remember shooting a cow, which fed us for half a year – luckily we had a couple of butchers staying with us at the camp at the time – and we'd often share what we had with the Aboriginal people, and they'd share with us.

'Another day we were out hunting, walking through the forest, knowing that we really needed a wild cow as we had so little food. An Aboriginal friend had given Dad a rifle and I had a .410-bore shotgun. I was terrified. If you come across a wild bull they can be super-aggressive and they must weigh over a tonne and are very, very dangerous. A .410 shotgun would be worse than useless if you came across one face to face; it's only good for shooting rats and birds and small animals. So, all the time I was thinking of different escape scenarios if we met one, like climbing up a tree. And then we stopped and saw a huge wild bull looking at us. Dad fired his gun and the scope just flew off. It might have been funny but we were so close, it wasn't. It could so easily have charged us and I knew, if it did, I had to make my shot count. But luckily, it turned away and ambled off.'

There were so many wild bulls in the area, sometimes they stomped into camp and the family could hear them breathing just centimetres away from the thin walls of the house. There was a huge commotion of roaring and bellowing one evening when two of the biggest, meanest bulls got into a fight, leaving much of the ground outside the house thoroughly churned up by their kicking hooves and massive horns.

It became a favourite evening pastime for Nick, Michael and Anya to go out under cover of darkness and creep up to a herd of wild cows to see how close they could get. 'We'd creep up like hunters might have done many years ago and Dad would make a mooing sound to attract them, and sometimes they'd moo back,' Anya says. 'I'd urge him to do it again, and so he would. It was just for fun, but then we might see a little cow and think maybe we could catch that for food. One night, we were so close but then Molly came bounding out and ran straight towards them and caused a massive stampede all around us. It sounded like an earthquake, all those heavy hooves bashing into the earth. We realised then how much danger we were in as there was a really big bull there with huge horns that looked like the leader. It stared at us, then started walking towards us and I thought we were goners. It was bound to charge us and then butt us. But Molly darted towards it and it took one look at her, and then turned and went in the opposite direction. She saved the day for us.'

Molly also proved handy in keeping the dingoes away. An Aboriginal friend had lost his dog to dingoes, but Molly seemed just big enough to give them pause. Anya found a dingo one day scavenging around looking for eggs, set Molly onto him and sent him packing.

'They were probably the same size, but dingoes can get spooked very easily,' Anya says. 'It got scared to see a big black dog running after it. Dingoes can be so unpredictable, you never quite know what they're going to do.'

The family also kept a peacock, a cockatoo and a goat called Banjo in their menagerie, along with pythons and moon snakes kept by Anya in various tanks. She was still the soft-hearted animal lover of the family but was gradually becoming more hard-headed about what they needed to do to survive. When they'd been at Goombaragin, they'd found a big side of beef in the freezer that they nicknamed Harold, and the first wild cow Nick shot they named Harold Junior in his honour. After he'd been butchered, Anya bleached his tail and hung it up on the washing line – a sight which shocked a few of their visiting city tourists – and thereafter used it as a fly and mozzie swat.

While she loved her waddle of ducks, and they'd follow her around the camp wherever she went, she resisted naming them as she knew, one inevitable day, they'd become valuable nutrition. As a result, when the time came, she took a deep breath and even volunteered to be the one to kill a couple. 'The ducks were smart and I felt I'd connected with them but you can't create as strong a bond with them as you can with other animals,' she says. 'They just see you as the feeder. And we really needed the meat. It's about survival. When it's you or them, that kind of survival instinct kicks in. I think it was a little bit hard the first time when I didn't really know what I was doing, but then it got easier.'

Anya tied up the legs of her first duck, hung it upside down and tucked its head under its wing to calm it. When she saw it had almost fallen asleep, she took a kitchen knife and wiped it smartly across its neck. It died shortly afterwards. 'After the first, it became a lot easier,' she says.

The pigs were a different challenge altogether. She was in charge of the pig pen and loved spending time there with the three pigs they started off with, which soon burgeoned to eleven.

'I would sit with them on the ground, and they would lay around me or the little ones would be in my lap,' she says. 'Pigs are highly intelligent and very social and loving animals. They all have distinctive personalities. You become their friend and they trust you, and they're good friends to you. One of them, Long Legs, was my favourite. She'd use my legs as a scratching pole and would sleep on my feet while I read a book or drew.'

But when Long Legs became bigger and fatter, there was no question that she would have to be the one to go. However tenderly Anya had felt towards her, she knew it made perfect sense.

'I think if we'd have stayed in England and I'd had a normal childhood, I would never have been game to end an animal's life,' Anya says. 'But out there, we had to survive. Of course, I felt a little bit sad, but I had to get over it. It was her or us. The reason she was there in the first place was to be killed and eaten. It just felt another part of life, to be honest. Dad killed her but then I did all the dirty work as he was so squeamish and there was no other way around it. It was quite simple really when you know basic anatomy. I gutted her and drained the blood and then boiled her in a rusty old bathtub we had, and then roasted her on a spit.

'I was 100 per cent fine with that as that was what she was there for, after all. Well, maybe 99 per cent. I did miss her.'

# EIGHTEEN

# CROCODILES, SHARKS AND SNAKES

THE MARSHLANDS, CREEKS AND mangroves of Banana Well were teeming with all manner of deadly animals and insects, which too often also found their way into the family's house.

King brown snakes, one of the most venomous species of snake in the world, were a particularly unwelcome, but regular, visitor. Attracted by the chickens and ducks being kept at the homestead, they'd often stick around to see what else they could find. Anya and Luda bolted from the outdoor toilet one afternoon, saying they'd seen a king brown hiding in the toilet cistern, probably in the hope of finding a frog or two, which might be there waiting for the moths that would swarm in whenever the light went on at night. Since the king browns were such territorial snakes, the family knew this intruder would have to be killed. Nick phoned their Aboriginal friend who'd lost his dog to a dingo to ask him what to do and was told he should pour boiling water into the cistern to flush it out.

Standing back, with Michael and Anya behind him, he gingerly lifted up the lid of the cistern with a stick, and then poured in the boiling water. Quick as a flash, the snake shot out of the cistern, up Nick's arm, over his shoulder and into the house.

'It happened in the blink of an eye,' Nick says. 'I didn't even have a chance to move. It was such a shock. But then I called my Aboriginal friend back and told him what had happened. He was unmoved. "Well, what would you do if someone poured boiling water on you?" he asked.'

Snakes were everywhere. One night, Nick and Luda stopped the car when they spotted a king brown in a death struggle with a huge monitor lizard in the middle of the road. They watched, fascinated, until suddenly the snake saw them, let go its grip and slunk away. The lizard rolled back onto its feet and waddled off, listing from side to side, punch drunk with venom. Nick and Michael discovered another king brown stretched out just inside the door of the generator house. They saw him in the nick of time and stepped over him. Then, armed with shovels, they tried to bash him but succeeded only in making him angrier as he disappeared, ready to reappear another day.

In the house itself, there were a few Stimson's pythons living in the roof and hanging around the rafters hunting for moths, and another one that had settled into a hole in the hessian under the sofa that managed to evade capture every time the family tried. Even when they were caught, however, they sometimes didn't stay captive for long. When Nick went to check on Anya one night, he found her fast asleep on her bed with the pillowcase that had held her pet python open at one end and empty.

'Oh, it must have come undone,' Anya offered sleepily when Nick woke her. 'I'm sure he'll be all right.'

There was a massive population of crocodiles in the area, too. Nick spotted a huge one once, about 500 metres away, not far off the shore. He walked 100 metres towards it to get a better look but was startled when suddenly it popped up right in front of him. While there were hundreds around, that was surely the sneaky, over-confident croc that had been terrorising the Beagle Bay mob who fished with handlines right on the edge of the creek. They sent one of their shooters to kill it for food but, despite being just fifty metres away, every one of his sixteen shots missed. In the end, they had to call the rangers, who set a trap in a little creek off the main one at Banana Well. The very next day, Nick and Michael went down to check things out and found a 3.8-metre croc inside the trap, with another one swimming all around it. The rangers then taped its mouth closed and transferred it to a crocodile park in Broome.

Another time, Nick caught a colossal barramundi and, finding it hard to haul in, slid down the mud bank in front of him to put his hands under it and push it up. As he was pushing, Luda was pulling on the line and, between them, they managed to flip it up onto land. But the bank was so slippery, Nick couldn't climb back up – until Luda started screaming that there was a crocodile just behind him. Then he managed, though he lost both his big toenails in the desperate scramble to safety.

Even the smallest critters could prove a nightmare. Michael and Nick pushed their way through thick mangroves early one morning, a distance from the camp, to try to find a good new fishing spot when suddenly Michael felt a sharp pain in his back, as if he'd been shot. Then another. And another. He looked up and saw he'd disturbed a nest of paper wasps hanging from a mangrove bush and they were now swarming around him and stinging him all over.

Nick also suffered an attack from a tiny creature. One night, around the bonfire, he picked up a piece of wood and later felt both his palms burning. He examined them and could see two little puncture wounds. Then his hands and both legs started swelling. The next day, he went to the clinic at Beagle Bay where he was given antihistamines. The swelling eased but, instead, a symmetrical rash broke out all over his body. This time, he consulted a pharmacist, who was fascinated, saying she'd never seen anything like it in her life. Since that day, whenever Nick has been bitten by anything, he suffers an outbreak of the same rash. 'It could have been a spider or maybe a centipede or anything really,' Nick says. 'But our biggest fear was that one of us would get really ill there or have an accident, and that would see us well and truly stuffed.'

Friendlier creatures would occasionally pass by, too. One day, Michael and Nick spotted a goat in the bush, so shot it and put it in the freezer. A few hours later, a neighbour called round, asking if they'd seen his pet goat. They tried to look concerned and assured him they'd look out for it.

Nature wasn't always the enemy, though. The guest swimming pool at the camp became murky with thousands of tadpoles and frogspawn so the family put a fish they'd freshly caught into the pool to see if it might eat them. The next morning when they went out, the water was crystal clear and the fish looked terribly bloated and pleased with itself. 'He looked as if nothing had happened,' Anya says. 'But I was really impressed by that. We then transferred it into our fish tank as we didn't want the tourists getting a fright.'

They also had their own vegetable garden and grew local bush apple, wild lemongrass, dragon fruit, watermelon and Kakadu bush plums along with the usual carrots, cabbages, peas, eggplant, tomatoes and chillies. They tried runner beans once, too, but the wild cattle took such a liking to them, they trampled the whole garden in their efforts to eat them, so those were quickly abandoned. Gardening was a dangerous pastime, though. King browns kept showing up while olive pythons were a constant threat to the chickens. The first one Nick caught – by using a sack – had three big lumps in it from the chooks it had swallowed.

Every night, Luda would sweep the ground flat so they could see the next morning if any unwelcome visitors had left tracks. Nick would constantly tell Anya not to walk around barefoot because of the snakes, but she did, regardless. She never panicked. One day in the pig pen, when she had to lift up the old satellite dish they used as a water trough to wash it and refill it with fresh water, she disturbed a king brown, but calmly asked her dad to fetch a gun to shoot it.

Anya would often wander around the place with Molly, Banjo their goat, any number of ducks and a pig or two in tow. Sometimes, she'd ride a quad bike to transport all the pig food down to the pen, although, when she hit a bump, she'd end up wearing the food instead. But whenever the family couldn't find her, they knew she'd be at the top of her favourite tree, a giant mahogany that had a clearing at the top, like a window to the world. There she'd sit for hours, watching the wild cattle in the distance, or flocks of bats, or birds.

'It's funny but I remember, growing up, that I always wanted to live on a farm,' Anya says. 'So being with all those animals was kind of my dream come true. But I never wanted it like that. It came at a great cost. I cried a lot, like *a lot*. I just felt so alone. I really missed my friends.

'At night, I'd look up at the stars and imagine they were my friends. I'd always try to hide my distress, though. Except one night, I found myself walking round and round in circles, thinking and thinking, and then I finally got up the courage to walk to my parents' unit and tell them how I felt. I remember saying, "Mum, Dad, I want to go home."

'And they said, "We know." And then we all cried.'

# NINETEEN
# DIAMONDS IN THE ROUGH

**IN SOME WAYS,** Michael was coping with the comparative isolation of Banana Well better than his sister. For a start, he was a year older, having turned sixteen on 6 February 2016, just before they were about to mark their first anniversary on the site. And his dad tried to keep him busy with as many projects as he could.

Good with his hands and blessed with a brain for mathematics and engineering, he took pleasure in completely different aspects of the place to Anya. One of his great joys was the rubbish dump where the local Aboriginal community discarded anything that no longer worked or they had no use for. Michael would call at the dump regularly to see if there were any treasures, and he'd rarely be disappointed. He rescued broken air conditioning units and repaired them, old lawnmowers which he also restored, and broken-down cars from which he scavenged parts to use for repairs to the family's own vehicles or those of visitors or locals.

'I found an old LandCruiser workshop manual, which meant I could work out what could go where,' he says. 'That was invaluable.

I'd then just strip some of the old bashed-up cars and take what we wanted. In the bush, you don't have access to real mechanics, so you have to teach yourself to do what needs to be done, and it was like having a hidden stash. I think the biggest lesson I learned was self-sufficiency.'

As well as fixing and building things around the camp and going around the units on a quad bike to sell families firewood to try to earn some cash, he'd also spend a lot of time fishing with his dad or with the other guests. Sometimes, it could be hair-raising. One time their little tinny was running aground in thirty centimetres of water and Nick and Michael jumped out to push it off the bank. Then Nick felt something large brush against his leg, and they both jumped smartly back in again. It was a giant crocodile.

Another time, they borrowed a bigger tinny from a local, who patched up and recycled old boats, to go out to a buoy about eleven kilometres offshore where the fishing was said to be excellent. Nick noticed the tinny had only a small anchor that he thought would be unlikely to hold it, especially in an area with tides of 10–11 metres, but they went regardless. Unfortunately, three-quarters of the way there, the engine broke down. 'We looked at the water and realised we probably had just four to five hours before the tide would turn and sweep us out into the ocean,' says Nick. 'And then no one would ever see us again. But we had two oars, so we pulled and pulled, but we were just going round and round and the shore wasn't getting any closer. Then we put in a massive, massive effort and finally got to the shore and then dragged the tinny along the sand back to the car. I think that's the closest we came to dying. But it didn't stop us. Michael fixed the engine, and we went back out the next week. There was nothing he couldn't fix.'

Nick would also take him on other little adventures from time to time. They'd usually go together on rescue missions, and often went walking together, too. But one time, on a trip to Broome for supplies, Nick's eye was caught by a book called *The Diamond Dakota Mystery* by Juliet Wills. He picked it up in the bookshop and started reading how it was a true war-time story of daring, mystery, luck and $20 million worth of diamonds, and how they were lost, found and lost again. His interest was piqued but the book was $27, and he had no cash to spare. The next time he visited, he picked up the book again to read a little more, and discovered the action was set on the Dampier Peninsula, close to Banana Well. So, he bought it.

Back home, both he and Michael pored over the pages. It was about a DC-3 plane that had been heading to the safety of Australia from Java in 1942, with 600 rough-cut diamonds on board in a brown-paper package. Close to Broome, it came under fire from Japanese planes on their way back from an air raid. The DC-3's Russian World War I flying ace, Captain Ivan Smirnoff, managed to land the damaged plane on a remote beach at Carnot Bay and, while some of the passengers died, eight survivors were eventually found. None of the diamonds, however, ever was.

'It was such an incredible story and we started talking about how close the crash site was to us, and that maybe we should go out there and see if we could find some of the missing diamonds,' Nick says. 'It was only forty kilometres away as the crow flies but it's a really remote place and you'd be driving off-off-road, and in soft sand, so it would take a long time. It's now called Smirnoff Beach, in memory of the pilot. While we knew it would be difficult, we thought we should give it a go.'

Michael was enthusiastic, too. 'We thought it would be a really long drive to get there, and it would be dangerous,' he says. 'It was sand-and-dirt track and if we got stuck, or broke down, we might never be able to get back. But it sounded like a really good idea and I was up for it.'

The first time the pair set out, they became hopelessly lost and had to return home after a few hours. The second time, they got lost again. The third time, they looked up the site on the internet in Broome, saw faint lines they imagined might be tracks, and drew a detailed map. They also decided to film their expedition. On their third attempt, they managed to make it all the way to Carnot Bay, where any sign of a track completely petered out. They thought they'd walk to the beach from there and put a couple of cans of Coke, a bottle of water and their snorkels in a bag and set off. They trudged a kilometre through the softest of sands in forty-degree heat under the burning sun and were just on the verge of giving up and returning to the car when Nick spotted something sticking up from the mud in the distance that looked like plane wreckage. They plodded another kilometre only to find it was a dead tree.

Father and son were, by now, starting to grow thirsty but they'd drunk everything they had with them. The temperature was still rising and both began feeling faint. But as they lumbered around the next corner, they could see, on the horizon, what looked like a wooden cross.

'Look!' shouted Nick. 'It's definitely a cross. Let's keep going!'

Four kilometres on, they finally reached it – a memorial cross with part of the aircraft's propeller attached, above a stone plinth with a plaque bearing the names of the two men, one woman and her one-year-old son who perished there. The book had described how the survivors hid behind rocks, so Nick and Michael had a look for diamonds under the rocks and bushes on the beach, and then waded into the ocean to snorkel around to search for anything glittering on the seabed. They soon came across the wreckage of the plane, encrusted with barnacles and coral and teeming with fish in every nook. They filmed their little underwater exploration.

Finding nothing precious, they finally gave up and began the long trek back to the car. As they slogged through the sand, it occurred to both of them this was the exact route two of the survivors took when looking for help.

'We thought this dehydration and exhaustion would have been exactly what they experienced all those years ago,' Michael says. 'You never know how many people die in those circumstances. We were looking for water as we went, just as I'm sure they did.'

Nick was of a similar mind. 'About halfway there, I started thinking while those two eventually made it, we might not,' Nick says. 'Our mouths were so dry, and we were exhausted, and our legs were dead. The only difference was that we knew just another couple of kilometres away, we had a car full of cans of Coke and twenty litres of water.'

By the time they reached the car, they were parched but, happily, the water and Coke tasted better than champagne. Their celebration was short-lived, however. On their way back, their vehicle suddenly stopped and started sinking in the sand. Both jumped out quickly to assess the situation.

'You can't help it, but your mind starts going,' Nick says. 'It's just a huge salt flat that you'd imagine the moon to look like and so dry and dangerous, and we were sinking in a mix of ocean and sand.

The tides are so big there, too, you can lose a car in minutes. I was thinking if we couldn't get out, you mightn't see anyone for three months in that area; it's so isolated. It would be hard to walk, too. I knew there was a community at Baldwin Creek, which was four hours away, but you'd have to carry so much water to make it there, it would be impossible.'

Instead, the pair let down the tyres, knowing that would give them a greater area of tread to help lift the wheels over the sand. That would normally mean lowering the tyre pressure from 30psi to 18. They let them down to 8psi, so there was virtually no air at all left in the tyres. Then they jumped back in, and Nick crunched into reverse.

'We had one chance of getting out of there, otherwise we would lose the vehicle to the ocean,' he says. 'And I slowly started to put the revs down and I felt the car move and come up and then I just put my foot down, and amazingly, it popped out of the sand. And I didn't stop madly reversing until we hit dry ground. But the problem was, we now had no air in the tyres, and we'd forgotten the air compressor. So, to stop the tyres overheating, we had to drive back home at like 10 to 15 kilometres an hour. It took about four hours.'

While they were both disappointed not to have found any treasure, they were relieved that they'd survived to tell the tale. 'I think I had this little fantasy in my head that I'd look and find a little wooden box containing diamonds or pearls from a Chinese adventurer who'd been big in the pearling industry,' says Michael. 'But then again, even if we'd found them, they might still have been the property of a bank or the government. Knowing our luck, with our visa situation, we might have been arrested for theft.'

It was well known that some Aboriginal people had found a few of the diamonds and traded them for smokes, food or drink.

One traditional owner told the pair they should look out for a tree with a chain around it and a padlock – that's where others had hidden a few. Another elder said some diamonds had been flung down Banana Well's own well and, while they briefly considered trying to drain it, they realised that would be impossible. But wherever Michael walked after that, he found himself looking for anything out of the ordinary.

They put their video up on YouTube and received messages from as far afield as the USA, from a history society focused on Pacific wrecks. They also received a note from the grandson of one of the plane's passengers. Nick 'Ashcroft' was then interviewed by an ABC radio station about the quest to find the diamonds. He and Michael returned to the wreckage site a few months later, too, when some visitors arrived from Broome and suggested a follow-up expedition – this time on quad bikes – which proved much less problematic.

The fame of Banana Well was growing all the time, and journalists from magazines and TV shows alike came out to report on the magnificent fishing at the camp, while some extremely wealthy guests also came to stay. One visitor, however, was very different from their regular kind of tourist. An elderly woman, she introduced herself as April and said she'd been trying to find the place where her grandfather, a legendary pastoralist pioneer of the Kimberley, had arrived on his ship, the *Heather Bell*, in 1882. She'd driven first to Beagle Bay but been unable to find where they might have docked.

'He wouldn't have sailed there, he would have sailed here,' Nick told her. 'Our place was the landing point of all the ships in that era. Come on, let me show you the place we call The Landing.'

April followed him down to the point and immediately burst into tears. 'This must have been it,' she said. 'How wonderful!

He came here at the age of twenty-one with nine employees, 2000 sheep, seven head of cattle and ten horses, and then travelled inland to pasture cattle and sheep. I can't believe I've found it.'

She told Nick that her grandfather, George Canler Rose, had arrived on the 472-tonne wooden barque and then led his brothers into the Kimberley to open the area up to livestock. Now she'd found his landing place, her dearest dream would be to erect a plaque to honour his memory.

Nick asked the Burrguk community leaders if that would be okay. They flatly refused. He then tried another tack. 'How about we put up two plaques,' he suggested. 'One to celebrate the founders of the Burrguk Aboriginal Corporation, and the other one for the white pioneers?'

They conferred and agreed. The deal was done.

So, on 3 September 2016, two memorial plaques commemorating the families that had played seminal roles in the history of the area were unveiled. One paid tribute to Tony Fitzgerald Ozies, Dominic Charles and Charlie Norman, the founding members of the Burrguk Aboriginal Corporation, and the other was in honour of the Rose family. More than forty descendants of each family came and stayed at Banana Well for an evening of storytelling and feasting at a long table Nick set up outside. April had told him not to worry about providing food, and her family, who turned out to be among the wealthiest people in Australia, sent over a mobile freezer with all the best cuts of meat for everyone, while the community roasted a kangaroo over the fire, and everyone joined in a competition to see who could cook the best damper.

'It was one of the loveliest evenings we had there,' Nick said. 'Everyone was so happy to have their ancestors recognised, and everyone got on so well. They all sat down and talked together and discovered that half of their families were related. It was fantastic to play a role in bringing these two groups together, and it's a memory that will always stay with me.'

Shortly afterwards, Nick, Michael and Anya called into Broome. By now, they'd all become self-conscious about how they looked, with their clothes increasingly shabby and their skin stained orange by pindan dust. 'Wow, man, you must be really out there doing stuff!' one man remarked as he surveyed them. Nick smiled and nodded; he was too embarrassed to admit they'd only come into town to do some shopping, and that's how they always looked.

Anya had rarely accompanied her dad on these outings as they were always nervous about being stopped by police and quizzed on their visas. This time, she found being there extremely difficult. 'I'd been living so out of civilisation that I kept slipping on the tiled pavements and floors,' she says. 'It was almost like I'd forgotten how to walk on a normal pavement again. I remember going to a normal toilet, too. And it just didn't feel right. I'd spent so long in the middle of nowhere that when I was somewhere, it felt all wrong.'

The family went through the supermarket and piled trolleys high with food to take back. Then Nick went off to check the news on the internet. In Australia, the Coalition had won the 2016 federal election, albeit with a reduced majority, under Prime Minister Turnbull. As for Russia, a Dutch-led prosecutorial team had just presented evidence that the missile that had downed MH17 had been launched from separatist territory in Ukraine with weaponry brought in from Russia and immediately returned there after the attack.

A few weeks later, in October 2016, as the family marked their second-year anniversary at Banana Well, their mood was gloomy.

Anya would spend hours with Molly, confiding how miserable she was, and Michael would often gaze wistfully at his old naval uniform, wondering if he'd ever get to wear it, or anything like it, ever again. They were all becoming tired of living so far off the grid, wondering if their exile would ever end.

The longer they stayed, the more Nick thought the end was nigh. One afternoon they even received a phone call from someone who said they were from the Lombadina Police HQ. 'Is that Nick?' the voice said down the line. 'Okay, it's time. We're coming to get you.' For the rest of that day, Nick and Luda sat motionless in the unit, in a cold sweat, waiting for the police to appear at the gate to arrest them. No one came, and they had to conclude it had just been a practical joke from someone who knew their circumstances. But that episode would haunt them.

The arrival of a savage rainy season, which transformed the ground around them into a swamp and cut them off from the rest of the world for a full three months – with the roads impassable both to and from the getaway, and the electricity cut off – didn't help one bit. Amid the saturation, Broome recorded its wettest December day on record, with 226 millimetres of rain brought in by Tropical Cyclone Yvette.

By the time Nick finally managed to leave Banana Well to replenish their supplies in Broome, the news from Russia was even worse. Russian press minister and former Putin advisor Mikhail Lesin, the man who founded the TV network Russia Today and who would have known plenty about the inner workings of the rich and powerful in the country, was found dead with a broken neck in a hotel room in Washington. The development sent a shiver down Nick's spine.

But even amongst themselves, tempers were fraying. Anya and Luda were arguing, and Nick could see the children were suffering from having no contact with anyone of a similar age and missing out so completely on their education. He'd tried to home-school both when they first arrived in Banana Well, but they'd resisted and eventually he'd given up. Now he was starting to think that maybe they should all just go back to Perth and face the music, however that played out. Luda, though, said she thought it would be best for them to stay up north. Suddenly, they were all bickering.

'We've got to do what's best for the kids,' Nick told Luda. 'We need to be getting them back home now, to some sense of normality. This isn't good for them. Anya's getting depressed and Michael should be finishing his education or making his own way in a workplace. They both need friends of their own age. It can't go on like this. It's gone on too long already.'

Eventually, they compromised. Nick said he'd been told by an Aboriginal friend about a remote beach 100 kilometres to the north where they could all go and stay in an empty house owned by a family member and be together and talk about what they should do next. When he and Luda told the children, they both looked relieved. They set their leaving date for 6 June 2017, two years and three months after they'd first arrived, and two years and seven months since they'd left Bunbury to go into hiding.

But in the interim, the intense wet, heat and lightning strikes had claimed another victim: the Nissan Patrol they'd set out in from Bunbury. Luckily, their Indigenous mate came to their rescue again. He had an old, red Toyota HiLux he was getting rid of, and he agreed to trade it for all the fish in their freezer. It wasn't an amazing bargain: the vehicle had no brakes, no suspension, and the roof was pitted with holes. Michael visited his beloved rubbish dump and scavenged parts to make it, if not safe, then a lot safer than it had been.

Even though Michael may have looked as though he'd been coping these past two years, the truth was he was only just managing to hold on. 'That whole experience definitely changed me,' he says. 'I have to be honest: being out of school and separated from society and civilisation must have done a lot of damage to me, really. I think it's important for kids to have friends and a social environment and I never had anyone. I think it's made me a much quieter person. Even to this day, I don't really have many friends.'

# TWENTY
# A FINAL TASTE OF PARADISE

THE MOOD IN THE old patched-up red rattler HiLux was sombre as the family set out from Banana Well on 6 June 2017. Nick tried to brighten the atmosphere by reminding everyone of the excitement they'd felt the first time they'd set off around Australia before handing themselves in to the authorities. This might be just like that, he cajoled – just the family relaxing in one of the most stunning spots in Australia and the chance to recuperate and regroup.

The drive, however, took much longer than it should have. The HiLux wasn't registered, and Nick's licence had expired, so they couldn't afford to take the one strip of bitumen up the Dampier Peninsula because of the risk of being stopped by police. Instead, they had to wind about on mostly unsealed roads.

Red Shells was a tiny Aboriginal community set on a beach on the National Heritage-listed coastal wilderness of Pender Bay, comprising one house, a shed and no permanent residents. The beach took its name from the millions of tiny blood-red crab shells scattered on the white sands fringing the turquoise ocean.

In the bright sunlight, they glittered scarlet and, together with the striking rust cliffs that lined the shore, the whole area glowed rose. The beach was accessible only by 4WD, so was mostly deserted, making it a haven for birdlife, fish, molluscs and humpback whales, which were just beginning their annual migration north from Antarctica.

They arrived just as the sun was setting and the sky was turning red. The scene filled Nick with a sense of foreboding, but he was determined not to give in to it. They unpacked the car and trailer and checked out the house. While basic, it was perfectly functional, with a small solar-powered system for electricity and water. They'd been assured by their friend they'd be perfectly safe here as he'd told the traditional owners that Nick was 'one of us'. With his skin stained by the pindan dust and darkened by the sun, he certainly looked the part.

Nick and Luda opted to sleep in the bed in the living room, Michael, by then seventeen, chose the shed, while Anya, sixteen, opted for a tent outside. Luda arranged their stockpile of food – rice, beans, cans of tomatoes and Spam, powdered milk, flour, curry powder – in the kitchen. The plan was to use these basics to supplement the fish they'd catch.

'The place was awesome,' Nick says. 'There was no one around us. We tried not to think about immigration or Russia and just went fishing, cooked damper and played games. But behind the scenes, I was planning. I was intent on persuading Luda we should go back to Perth and front up to immigration, but I realised even the thought was making her anxious. I saw Anya becoming more alone because she wasn't spending enough time with her mother, and I didn't want Michael facing the prospect of turning eighteen and still being unlawful. While he was a minor, he was reasonably safe, but once he passed that birthday . . . So, I was nervous about putting us back into the lion's den, but in the meantime I was doing my best to pretend to be happy and carefree.'

Not everyone was fooled. Michael understood what his dad was trying to do, but he wasn't convinced. 'The idea was that we'd have our final happy moment before we handed ourselves in, a final taste of paradise,' he says. 'And Red Shells *was* a beautiful place. But again, I have to be honest: I didn't like it. I was living in a tin hut and I didn't have much to do. We had hardly any power, so I just had some battery left on my phone, and I listened to the same songs I'd downloaded back in Bunbury all that time ago over and over on repeat. I knew every word to Chas & Dave's "Snooker Loopy" and to my favourite Johnny Cash song, "Folsom Prison Blues" . . . *I'm stuck in Folsom prison, and time keeps draggin' on* . . . I listened to that song hundreds and hundreds of times and it felt like it had an additional meaning for me. At Red Shells, it felt like the walls were closing in, just like it had felt on our last days in Bunbury. We were starting to lose hope for a good outcome. I wasn't sure what our next steps would be, and you couldn't plan anything.'

Likewise, Anya was in a poor frame of mind, worried that the family's money was running out and that food here would be harder to come by. 'We were on our own now,' she says. 'Our relationships had got kind of strained. I'd argued a lot with Mum, and it felt as though things were crumbling. I think I was a difficult teenager, but perhaps ten times more than most kids because we were in these desperate circumstances and we were struggling, which kind of makes you different. I was very troublesome at times, even selfish. I blamed everyone for us being there.'

217

Her relationship with her mum became increasingly tense and while Nick constantly tried to keep the peace, he was becoming less successful with each day that passed. Michael and Anya didn't talk much, and she had no idea how he was feeling about their situation. Everyone seemed to be bottling up their feelings.

'But one day, I caught my dad looking at me with such sadness in his eyes,' Anya says, tears now running down her face at the memory. 'And I looked back at him with sadness, too. Although, back then, we never really opened up to each other, I think, at that moment, we knew exactly what the other was feeling.

'I have to tell the truth. That was the point [when] I started to self-harm. It was only a little bit, just once or twice. I found a rusty old knife on the beach. I'd had a friend in Bunbury who was struggling, and I learnt it from her. I didn't really understand it, but I thought this is what people do when they're sad. I was very lonely. Of course, we had each other, but I still felt so alone.'

Anya often heard her dad trying to persuade her mum they should leave and return to Perth and, as the first week passed at Red Shells, his pleas seemed to be gaining a new urgency. They assumed even more of an edge that first weekend when a group of twelve children arrived suddenly in a Sea Scout troop to do exercises on the beach and learn how to launch flares. It was a shock seeing so many white faces, and Nick noticed, painfully, how Michael and Anya at first shied away from speaking to their young visitors.

'It made me realise, even more strongly than before, that I had to get them back to some sort of normality,' Nick says. 'Seeing them so unsure around other people showed me very forcefully that we were in the wrong place.'

218

The visitors, all aged between twelve and fourteen, slept on camp beds in the shed, alongside Michael, and gradually Nick could see his children warming up to them and start chatting. That Saturday night, the family also joined in a game the kids were playing, where they sat in a big circle and passed around a stick with only the holder allowed to speak. For the Strides, it was hard to follow exactly what was happening, but they laughed and joked along with everyone else. It warmed Nick's heart to see his children smiling again.

When the Sea Scouts left, however, the emptiness of their lives became even more stark. Michael had enjoyed watching the Sea Scouts; they'd reminded him of his cherished days in the Sea Cadets.

'I did like being around them,' he says. 'It did make me think of the Sea Cadets again, but I realised then that I could never go back to them. So, I took out my uniform one last time, built a fire with some wood from the beach, and burnt it. It was sad, but I had to face up to those days being finished. I remember thinking, *I'm sorry, I'm sorry to do this, but I have no choice. It has to be done.* We had no rubbish tip or anything there so everything had to be burnt, and that was the final fate of my uniform, too.'

As the family began their second week at Red Shells, Nick reached a decision. He was going to tell the department where they were, and surrender. He emailed them to that effect, then sent another email to Michaelia Cash (whom he assumed was still the Assistant Minister for Immigration and Border Protection), who'd been the last person he'd applied to for a Ministerial Intervention. To her, he outlined the desperate straits the family were in and appealed yet again for an intervention.

Nick had been off the grid for so long, however, he had no idea she'd moved off the portfolio to become the Minister for

Employment. Her former boss, Scott Morrison, had also moved; he was now the Treasurer. The new head honcho in immigration was a relatively new cabinet member, Peter Dutton. Nor was Nick aware that the Australian government was facing a class action against them concerning asylum seekers kept at the Manus Island detention centre. The government had just agreed to compensate 1900 current and former asylum seekers a total of $70 million plus costs, in what was thought to be the largest-ever human-rights-related settlement.

Instead of receiving return emails, saying officers were on their way to pick them up, Nick received nothing from either the department or Cash. 'I think by then we were dead to them,' he says. 'We had nowhere to go, no food and no money. We had no future, nothing. We were dead.'

# TWENTY-ONE
# THE BEACH

**AFTER TWO WEEKS AT** Red Shells, Nick realised it was time to leave. Although he'd heard nothing back from either Perth or Canberra, he knew that if immigration officials did turn up to arrest him and his family as fugitives, he risked the freedom of the people who'd helped them.

The question was, what to do next? They'd all but run out of options. They knew their decrepit old HiLux wouldn't get them all the way back to Perth, and handing themselves in to the police in Broome probably didn't make much sense, either. The danger was that the police could turn them away and then they'd be homeless and broke in the town. It was one thing being homeless and broke in the bush, where you could survive on fish, favours from locals and savoir faire. It was quite another living on the cold, hard streets. Nick knew his family couldn't survive that.

While Red Shells was certainly remote, Nick now changed course and came up with a plan to go even further off the grid – to an isolated beach in the middle of nowhere, where no one ever lived or could offer to help, and where no tourists were allowed to visit.

He traced the route to this new spot, which would take them on dirt tracks and rutted crossings, over sand dunes and across vast empty horizons. Then he plotted the latitude and longitude of their destination and emailed the exact coordinates to immigration officers in case they ever did respond and wanted to show up to claim their prisoners. He followed that up with an email pleading for help from every Australian politician whose email address he could find. 'We felt that if someone didn't help or come and get us, we could well be living out there for the rest of our lives,' Nick says. 'It wasn't the most pleasant of thoughts.'

So, on the afternoon of Wednesday 21 June 2017, Nick, Luda, Michael and Anya packed all their possessions and their dwindling supplies of food and water into the car and trailer, and gloomily climbed in, with Molly jumping up to join them. No one knew what to expect, and it was anyone's guess as to how this latest adventure would end.

'We didn't want to ask anyone for help, and we didn't want to be a burden on anyone,' Michael says. 'But it was another really low point for us as a family. We decided to drive late in the day so we'd avoid the police and not get pulled over, and we didn't want anyone to know that we'd left or know where we were going. It was a strange feeling. We were going to be driving into the unknown and we didn't know what was going to happen to us when we got there.'

Anya, too, was glum. 'Dad said it would be our final adventure, but it didn't feel exciting at all like an adventure should feel. It just felt grim and desperate.'

The HiLux seemed to have absorbed their melancholy. Nick turned the key, and it refused to start. He tried again, and again, with no joy. Everyone clambered back out and he and Michael peered under the bonnet. Eventually they discovered the problem: a split in the fuel hose. They used whatever they could find to patch it up until the car finally came back to life. 'It was as if it didn't want to leave either,' Nick says. 'That car felt part of the family. It always stood by us. It was knackered and dirty just like us, but always trustworthy.'

By the time they were ready to set off, the sun had almost set in its usual reds and golds, and then night came on quickly. The dirt track was so furrowed and potholed, Nick was forced to drive no more than 10km/h, as the car shook and clanged with the effort. Anya had Molly on her lap in the back and stared out of the window. Michael also peered out, shivering. 'It was really spooky,' he says. 'It was pitch black with no moon and this thick fog came down to envelope us. We couldn't believe it. How come a fog descended on this very day? It felt so surreal.'

After driving for about two hours, they arrived at the beach Nick had settled on. It was so far off the beaten track, it didn't even seem to have a name. The family decided, henceforth, it would be known simply as The Beach. They drove up and down for a while longer, working out a good place to make camp. When they came across a rocky ledge, Nick hoisted the main tent for himself, Luda and Anya, while Michael pitched his own one-man tent beside it and they made a bed for Molly under the trailer. They built a firepit with rocks, collected enough firewood so they could keep it going twenty-four hours a day, and designated a patch in the bush where they'd go to the toilet, always with a shovel in hand. Then they all went to sleep. There was nothing else to do.

223

The next day, Nick presented Anya with two gifts – a book that he'd bought her in Broome with the family's last few dollars, and her own tiny tent. She burst into tears. 'He didn't have much money, but he bought me *Harry Potter and the Philosopher's Stone* and a tent to try and make me happy,' she says. 'I used to sit in the backseat of the HiLux, which was the only place you could get away from the flies, and read it. He's such a good dad. But I cried a lot at The Beach, mostly at night when no one else could hear me, or I'd go for a walk in the dark and cry then. I was often scared there. I didn't eat for like a week at first as I was too nervous to go to the bush toilet in the wilderness like that.'

Gradually, life fell into a routine. In the morning, everyone would clean the camp, so the sand that blew in didn't build up too much, brush the sand out from inside the tent and check for bugs. Then Nick, Michael and Anya would take their homemade spears – fashioned from wood with a sharpened metal rod affixed to the top – and hunt for rock cod and octopus in the rockpools at low tide. Nick and Michael would go off in the HiLux to gather firewood, while other vital daily chores included collecting seawater in buckets so that, after dark, they could heat up the water and wash.

A small solar panel charged up batteries for the phone, a light and their small radio. In the evenings, they all sat around the fire, with Luda cooking the rice and any fish caught, with the occasional delicacy being damper dipped in oil or canned baked beans. After eating, they'd all sit with a scrap of paper and a pencil and do quizzes that Nick would make up and mark. He'd always have a trick task, like, 'Draw a Sopwith Camel', or a question about the kids' animated TV show *Winx Club* that only Anya could answer.

The last thing they did of an evening, when the fire had all but burnt out, was to place a log upright in the centre of the firepit so it would slow burn with hot embers under the ash.

As before, the days began merging into one and it was soon hard to keep track of how long they'd been there. In some ways, it already felt like a lifetime. Sometimes, it was hard to imagine any other world beyond this remoteness. But always in the background was the thought of the Russians and Australian immigration. As a result, perhaps around six weeks into their stay at The Beach, Nick decided he should nip into Broome to check whether the department or any politicians had replied to his emails. It was an elaborate exercise. With the HiLux so flagrantly unroadworthy, he and Michael devised a plan in which they'd drive off-road to get as close to town as possible, then hide the car in the bush and hitch-hike the rest of the way. After they'd visited town, they'd hitch-hike back out and pick up the car. Drivers always stopped to give them a ride. After all, they were just about the only people anyone had ever seen hitch-hiking on that stretch of road.

Sure enough, Nick had received an email from the department. He opened it gingerly, hoping against hope it would contain news of a reprieve. It didn't. Instead, it was simply a terse note telling him to stop emailing them. 'I was stunned,' Nick says. 'That was it. It was simply unbelievable. I couldn't believe that's all they had to say to me. But we knew they were just biding their time till we came back, and then we'd be in exactly the same position again.'

That night, back on The Beach, he lay down and gazed at the stars, which were exceptionally bright out there, and waited for a shooting star that he could make a wish on. That became his nightly routine. Only then would he sleep. 'Nature's clock is sunrise, sunset and the tides,' he says. 'There were sometimes surprises, too. I'd go on long walks with Michael and on one of those jaunts, we discovered a large sandy area, an ancient seabed and lagoon littered with Aboriginal artefacts, flint spearheads and honing stones. It was incredible.

'Those weeks of barefoot hikes in searing heat and scorching pindan sand made the soles of my feet as tough as old leather, but the cracks on the side of my heels were deep and painful. We still had a box of tools and a battery sander, and that worked wonders on my feet, though Luda was not impressed.'

Anya would also go walking, always barefoot, alone with Molly through the early-morning mist, to explore the rock pools and watch the turtles and octopus. Her feet also became so tough that she could walk over the sharpest oyster shells without sustaining a single cut, while Molly would jump into the pools and chase the fish and sometimes, much to Anya's terror, sharks. Anya would also dig for hermit crabs, which they'd use for bait, and would swim out to a rock in the ocean and dangle a hand line into the water. She liked carrying her spear but no matter how many times she plunged it into the water hoping to impale a rock cod, she was never successful.

She hated The Beach. 'If I had to describe how I felt about being there, I'd say I was dying inside every day,' she says. 'I was miserable, lonely and desperate. We were all unhappy. I hated so much about it. I hated the bush toilet and I hated having to wash out of a bucket. I would always hide behind the car when I did it as I had a lot of body issues. One time, I didn't brush my hair for three months. It seemed like a waste of time. After a while, I also became reluctant to clean my teeth as I knew we were running out of water and it seemed such a waste. I was getting wild and I started feeling paranoid. I wasn't in a good place. The boredom and loneliness eat away at you.

'We'd often sit around the campfire and stare at the sky to spot shooting stars and one night I looked up and thought I could see the shape of God, even though I don't believe in Him. But that night, I just prayed and prayed. I said, "Please help us. Get us out of here. *Please!*"'

# TWENTY-TWO
# ANOTHER CHOICE

THE BEACH WAS, in truth, a brutally harsh place, with the pindan absorbing so much heat from the blistering sun each afternoon that it was often too painful to walk on. Every day seemed hotter than the last, and the only available shade came from an old, tattered bedsheet they'd strung up. There was never any breeze – just still air filled with flies, the unrelenting chirping of crickets and the endless crashing of waves on the shoreline. The only thing that broke the monotony was the sound of passing whales breaching.

Water was a constant and urgent problem. Driving the HiLux off The Beach towards Broome was always a risk because of the possibility of being stopped by police. And the task of hiding the car, hitching into town and then lugging back half a dozen twenty-litre containers of water in searing heat was exhausting and stressful.

Nick and Michael, at one stage, had the idea of trying to dig for fresh water, but after digging a hole halfway to China, they had to concede it was futile. Then, on the way to town one day, disaster struck.

'The leaf spring suspension broke on the car, it just snapped,' Michael says. 'At that moment, we thought, *Okay, that's us finished. We're done.* We were stuck in the middle of the bush and had no transport. But then we had the most tremendous luck. We found an old, burnt-out 1950s Holden that had obviously been dumped maybe thirty, forty or fifty years before. I took a spring off it and we put that inside our car as a makeshift type of spring. It worked! We managed to get out of there, and that prolonged the life of the car.

'But everything else we had was starting to deteriorate, too. Our tents were sun bleached and torn and our camp was in such a pitiful state, it looked like a refugee camp in a war zone. Then we went to rescue a woman – God knows where she'd come from – who'd got stuck in her car and I noticed that even when I put my foot down hard in the HiLux, it had no power at all. We were truly on our last legs, and in our situation, this could be life or death.'

But however strong the realisation that they couldn't survive on The Beach for much longer, they couldn't see any way out. After four months living there, Anya started believing they'd be there forever.

'That scared me a lot,' she says. 'I thought, *I'm going to be older and I'll still be here.* I thought that every single day. I had no idea how long we'd been there. Time just doesn't exist when you're in survival mode. It just seems to stretch forever. I bottled up all my feelings and it became really bad. I don't know where it came from, but suddenly I'm like, *I don't really want to live anymore,* and I got flashes of my death. I did think about killing myself. I wasn't going to do it; I just thought about it. I asked myself, *What's better than suffering?* I couldn't find a way out and I didn't want to continue being so sad.

'I was only a child, and I didn't know how to control my anger and my distress, and I was just a bit of a mess. I knew Dad was hurting, too. One minute, we'd be fighting or bickering and then the next minute we'd have our arms around each other, and everything was okay again. He looked at the sunset every afternoon until it went dark and would just stare out into the open, empty world. Sometimes, I'd go and stand next to him, and we'd hold hands.'

Nick and Michael's habit of going on long walks together continued, and often they walked up to twenty kilometres over the rocks and through thick bush in their bare feet just to kill time, more than anything. But these walks also gave them valuable father-son hours. They talked through their predicament and discussed every possible way out of it that they could think of; they'd pull each plan apart, examine every fragment of it, then put it back together before invariably discarding it as unworkable.

Luda was still resisting going back to Perth, dreading the possibility she might be sent back to Russia, and this was everyone's biggest fear. She was adamant they should stay on The Beach, despite the cost to everyone's physical, mental and emotional health. That viewpoint was understandable in her position. But while Nick was obviously sympathetic to it, he felt that now they really didn't have any choice: they had to leave, and soon. They'd run out of rice, they'd run out of beans and now they were close to running out of water again. Everything they owned had become threadbare and torn and even their car was surely on the verge of conking out. They had to get out, he insisted, because trumping all other considerations, it was imperative they return Michael and Anya to civilisation.

During the long walks with Michael, Nick spoke openly of his conviction that it was time to leave, and of his misery and frustration around Luda's refusal to see sense. Michael had his own view. 'My opinion at the time was that we had to do whatever we had to do to survive, and that meant leaving The Beach,' Michael says. 'And if Mum didn't want to go, if she wanted to hold us back, and starve us to death, well, we'd still have to go. We had to do whatever it would take to get Anya out of there. We could see how much of a toll it was taking on her.

'So, if Mum still refused to go, then we'd have to leave her there. Of course, that was obviously the last thing I wanted to do; no son should ever abandon his mother. But it was either that or abandon ourselves. We really had no choice. Staying there was simply unsustainable. So, Dad and I came up with a bunch of plans, something for every eventuality. These things might never happen, but we had to think of them anyway, just in case. Emergency plans if things went wrong, like, if she tried to stop us, maybe we'd sneak some stuff into the car and then take off. But the first choice was always that we persuade her to come with us, back to civilisation. And we tried and tried and tried.'

It was in the middle of all that, one day during their fifth month of living on The Beach, that the family were startled to see an older man drive up in a late-model 4WD campervan. It was a shock to see another human being in their world. He parked, then approached them with a wave and a smile. He was clearly taken aback, however, by how dishevelled and gaunt they looked.

After the man gave Molly some chicken, and then the family some beefburgers, Nick says it was like a dream to taste proper food again.

'But the whole thing made me realise how far we'd fallen. He obviously realised we were in dire straits and also gave us some water. But it was at that point I realised we really couldn't go on like this any longer. Everything, and everyone, was falling apart.'

The next morning, the man wandered back over to say goodbye. He was off, he told them – he'd just been making a pitstop on his journey. But as soon as he got close to the HiLux, Molly started barking. He leant over to pat her, and she lunged at him, her teeth bared. The man jumped back, but too late. To the family's horror, he was now oozing blood from a chunk Molly had taken out of his leg. It seemed that it wasn't only the human inhabitants that The Beach was driving mad.

'And that was it, it was like Molly had finally gone bush,' Nick says. 'Once she'd bitten someone like that, she was no longer safe to be around. It was yet another turning point.'

Luda was still saying she wanted to stay on at The Beach, still worried sick about a banishment to Russia. Nick was beside himself. 'I could absolutely understand her terror,' he says. 'But we had to think of our children. They came first. Their whole lives were ahead of them. They had the right to grow up like normal children, the right to live like regular people. I loved Luda dearly and had tried to protect her for so long, for so many years. Together with the kids, she was my life. We'd been through so much together and I couldn't imagine ever being without her. But now I really had no choice. I had to cast my feelings aside and take our kids to safety. If she still refused to leave The Beach, however, the thought of abandoning her was heartbreaking. It was a hellish choice. Yet at the end of the day, it wasn't mine to make. It would have to be the kids who made that final choice.'

That evening, he took Michael on a short walk along the seashore. It brought back so many memories of giving the children a momentous choice once before – back in Bunbury, just over three years ago, when they were deciding whether to acquiesce to being sent back to the UK or to go on the run. He pushed the thought back.

Finally, he said to his son, this was decision time. They'd talked this situation through so many times before but now Michael had to choose. If his mother still refused to leave The Beach, what did he want to do: stay with her, or leave her behind? It was the kind of call, Nick knew, that no kid should ever have to make. But he had to ask.

Next, he wandered back to the camp, and found Anya sitting by the fire alone. Nick asked her to come for a walk, during which he presented her with the same choice. 'I'm sorry to ask you this, Anya,' he said. 'But do you want to stay with your mum, or do you want to go, even if it means leaving her behind?'

The most shocking thing, when Nick thought about it later, was how quickly both kids said the same thing. Without a moment's hesitation, they each said they wanted to go. And if their mum wouldn't go with them, then they were more than ready to leave her behind. 'We have to go, Dad,' Michael had said. 'We just can't stay here, we can't. We have to save ourselves.'

# PART FOUR
# THE END OF THE ROAD

# TWENTY-THREE
# THE END OF THE ROAD

**IT WAS THE MOST** surreal situation. After three years and eighteen days of living hand-to-mouth on the run in one of the most remote frontiers of outback Australia, and spending the last five months nearly starving to death on a deserted beach, the ragtag little group was being surrounded by cheering children. None of them could quite believe it. It was probably the most bizarre moment of the whole experience.

Luda had finally agreed, at the last minute, to leave The Beach with Nick and the kids, knowing that they were, by now, out of food, almost out of water and completely out of hope that anyone would ever come to collect them. Nick had also told her that, even if she didn't agree, he would still have to take Michael and Anya away with him back to safety.

So, it wasn't a particularly happy group that arranged to leave The Beach for the last time. Nick had emailed forms to the department lodging yet another application for a Ministerial Intervention, and heard back that the department had granted the family bridging visas while Minister Dutton considered intervening. But as they started packing up, the two adults were grim-faced, Michael, seventeen, looked exhausted and Anya, sixteen, was heartbroken at the thought of having to say goodbye to Molly, her constant companion since Bunbury, as she was now too dangerous to be around other people in a city. The HiLux was on its last legs but, happily, Nick had seen an ad on the internet the last time he was in Broome for campervan relocations by a company called Wicked Campers. For the nominal fee of $1 a day, plus fuel, you could drive a campervan from Broome back to Perth to help the rental company relocate its vehicle. With the last speck of power on his mobile, he called them and yes, they had a van free which needed a driver. Could he come by the next day to pick it up?

On Saturday 18 November 2017, it was agreed that Nick and Michael would drive the HiLux almost to Broome, leave it in the bush and hitch-hike into town as per usual to pick up the campervan, leaving Luda and Anya behind to pack everything worth taking into the trailer. Everything went well until Nick and Michael arrived at Wicked's office, fondly imagining they'd be given a sleek, ultra-powerful, elegant and shiny vehicle. Instead, they received one that had been painted up to resemble the brightly coloured Mystery Machine from *Scooby-Doo*.

They drove back to the HiLux and Michael stayed with the Mystery Machine while Nick took the old banger back to The Beach to pick up the others. He hitched the trailer onto the back and they set off down the track. 'I remember thinking, *All we've got to do now is get back to Michael*,' says Nick. 'Then we're good to go. But I think I was so desperate to get off that beach, I was driving too fast, maybe 100km/h, and – oh, my God! – one of the rear wheels flew off. I was fishtailing all over the place with the trailer swerving behind me and, in the mirror, I could see the wheel rolling down the track behind us. Eventually, I managed to stop, and I put the wheel back on. But I could see it had ripped off through the studs, so I knew it could come off again any time. As a result, I had to drive very, very slowly, which was infuriating as I just wanted to get back to Michael.'

When they finally arrived, they realised they had far too much stuff to pack into the Scooby-Doo van, so they left their tent and other pieces of camping equipment they knew they wouldn't be able to sell on the side of the road. Michael drove the HiLux deep into the bush to dump it there. Then they continued in the Mystery Machine back into Broome to sell what they could to raise money for fuel for the journey to Perth. Someone at the campground bought most of it, including their chainsaw and Esky, although he looked at them as though they were aliens. 'You can't blame him, really,' Nick says. 'We were absolutely covered in pindan dust and it's so fine, it penetrates the skin, so we were completely orange. It took weeks and weeks to get back to our normal colour.'

Next came the sad mission of handing Molly over to a pet-rehoming charity. Anya was devastated and hugged her as if she'd never let go until Nick managed to ease her gently from his daughter's arms. 'That was probably one of the hardest things I've ever had to do,' Anya says. 'I wanted to know that she'd be safe and well cared for. I knew I had to let her go in order to get back to civilisation and survive myself. When the time came to say goodbye, I remember lifting her chin up and kissing her on the nose and walking away. It's haunted me ever since.'

As they all climbed back into the Mystery Machine to set off on the long drive to Perth and whatever horrors awaited them there, a gaggle of small children squealed with delight at the sight of the colourful van with their favourite cartoon character on it and gathered to wave them farewell. Nick, Michael and Anya smiled at them and waved back. No one seeing them would ever have had any idea of the horrendous ordeal they'd just been through.

'The first time I saw the Scooby-Doo van, I thought that it was really funny,' Anya says. 'But then I found it really embarrassing. Everyone looked at us, and I remember waving but then ducking my head, hiding. It was just the most embarrassing thing.'

Nick drove out of town, then drove and drove. He wanted to put as much distance between them and The Beach as he could in case Luda changed her mind and decided she wanted them to turn around and go back. The atmosphere was tense.

'How long do we think we spent at The Beach?' Nick asked the family, an hour into the journey, in an attempt to slice through the gloom.

'Three months?' Anya ventured.

'Nine months?' suggested Michael.

Luda said nothing.

'Well, I reckon it was somewhere in between,' Nick said, trying to force a laugh. 'Maybe five months. And a bit.'

He drove two days without sleep, only stopping for fuel. At that point, he said he just had to stop and have a nap. He pulled over, fell asleep and then woke with a start, and turned the engine back on. 'But Dad,' Anya said, 'you've only been asleep for five minutes.' In retrospect, he thinks he was delirious from lack of sleep and, as the sun came up that morning, he lost the sight in his right eye. Everything went blurry and he could no longer focus. It terrified him and finally persuaded him he had to stop and sleep for a few hours.

By the time they hit Bunbury, everyone felt relieved but also anxious again, because none of them knew what would be waiting for them. This could be that dreaded moment when Nick, Luda and the children would be detained ahead of deportation. They stayed with their friends, the Delanes, for a couple of days, then dropped the Scooby-Doo van back in Perth and went to visit the department, which had, in their absence, changed into the Department of Home Affairs. It gave them a further four-week bridging visa. Afterwards, they rented a small two-bedroom house at a reduced rent in return for doing some renovations to the place.

Delane says it was tremendous to see them again, but they'd changed in the interim. 'Michael had grown into a real young man and Anya a young lady. Nick was just the same, and I only saw Luda briefly. But I could see the toll the stress had taken on them all, particularly Anya. She was going through those difficult teenage years and having no base and no friends must have been so difficult for her.'

But being stuck back on the merry-go-round of visa issues was doing no one any good. 'This was one of the worst times because we were just going round and round in circles,' says Nick. 'They couldn't resolve the situation, we couldn't resolve the situation and none of us knew what to do. It felt like we were heading for a destructive future. It was amazing, too, that coming back into society proved so difficult for us all. Whoever would have thought living normally would be such a tough challenge?

'I think we all found it so hard to pick up where we left off. Nothing could make up for those years away. We were all under huge stress. Anya went back to school, but she started having panic attacks and I'd have to go in and pick her up. I think she couldn't cope being around lots of people again, all talking and laughing, after so long on her own. She really struggled.'

Anya remembers sitting at her desk every day, unable to stop crying. Her friends had all grown older and taller, and she felt like she'd been left behind. 'I'd kind of forgotten how to communicate with people because we'd been on our own so long,' she says. 'I started avoiding human contact because I was so scared of talking to people. I developed a terrible stutter and when I did talk, I'd stumble over my words a lot and get embarrassed. I became a real loner and would often run out of the classroom crying and people would wonder what was wrong with me. But it was a different world and I found it so difficult.'

Michael was too old to go back to school, so he started working with his dad doing small renovations on other people's houses. They didn't have a work visa but there was no other way they could survive. Michael felt lost.

'It was a very awkward time,' he says. 'I'd just come back from three years of living in the bush and it kind of felt a bit as though I was a soldier coming back from the frontline, and not knowing how to adjust. Of course, I can't compare myself to a soldier, but it just felt like we'd been though all these traumatic events, and they had changed us, and I no longer knew my way in life or how to interact with my old friends. My former classmates had been going to school all that time I'd been away and nothing much had changed in their lives, but I felt like I'd aged twenty years. I don't want to sound arrogant at all, but I didn't even know who these people were anymore, and I'm sure they felt the same about me. It was taking me a while to re-integrate into society.'

Luda, too, felt the pressure and went, at that stage, to go and live with a friend. 'It was desperately sad,' says Nick. 'But I felt that immigration had put us under so much stress, it had effectively destroyed our marriage.' Nick and Luda have been estranged ever since.

Time dragged on and the indecision began to feel suffocating. Christmas was a sombre affair; no one felt as if they had anything to celebrate. The New Year brought more bad news, both at home and abroad. In March 2018, in the little central Queensland town of Biloela, a Sri Lankan asylum-seeker family, including two Australian-born children, were raided by the Australian Border Force when their visa expired by a single day and they were taken into detention in Melbourne, 1500 kilometres away. Nick followed the case in horror.

At the same time, in Russia, things seemed to be heating up. Putin won a fourth term in office that wouldn't expire until 2024. Also in March, a former Russian KGB agent who'd been exposed as a double agent with the UK's intelligence services was mysteriously poisoned, along with his daughter, in the British city of Salisbury. Both Sergei Skripal and Yulia were admitted to hospital in a critical condition after being contaminated with the Russian-developed Novichok nerve agent. Authorities treated the case as attempted murder, although both father and daughter pulled through and were able to tell their tale. British Prime Minister Theresa May said Russia was responsible for the attack and announced the expulsion of twenty-three Russian diplomats in retaliation. To Nick, the incident confirmed all his fears about how easy it might be for Russian agents to take revenge in Britain on anyone considered an enemy.

'That became a huge case in the UK that captured everyone's imagination, with the pair being found unconscious on a park bench and sparking a huge scare,' Nick says. 'It was even made into a TV mini-series in 2020, *The Salisbury Poisonings*, that became a massive hit. But for me, it was personal. The news of the Novichok hit came as a huge shock, but it felt like vindication. It meant I was right to resist being sent back to the UK.'

Two months later, Shuvalov's six years as First Deputy Prime Minister came to an end, but then he was given another huge job: the position of Chairman of VEB.RF, Russia's national economic development institution. His influence wouldn't be waning anytime soon. Even though Nick tried not to think about Russia, it was hard to ignore. The FIFA World Cup, with Shuvalov as head of its organising committee, was kicking off on 14 June 2018 and global anticipation was at fever pitch.

By that July, Anya's panic attacks were growing worse, and developing into severe anxiety and depression, and she started getting eczema all over her body. While doctors prescribed powerful medication, nothing seemed to help.

Anya remembers it as an extremely dark period in her life. 'My stress was probably higher than it had ever been, everything confused me and I was a wreck,' she says. 'Even things like eating at McDonald's had a bad effect on me, as I wasn't used to that kind of food. And my eczema just enveloped me and swallowed me up. I genuinely thought I looked like a monster. I hated myself. I didn't want to live anymore. I hated every second of it.

'I was writhing in so much discomfort and ended up bed-bound for six months. Oh, my God, the eczema kept me up all day and night and I never had a single moment where I didn't itch or feel uncomfortable. Eventually I started having panic attacks and screaming, "Make it stop! Make it stop!" And one day Dad cried with me as I screamed and he said, "I'm so sorry, I'm so sorry", and he took me to hospital.'

With Anya struggling to breathe, the surgeons sedated her, then knocked her out completely with medication. Nick, beside himself with worry, collapsed at her bedside. 'It felt like my whole life had ended,' he says. 'For Anya, I think it was just a culmination of everything that had been going on, compounded by the intense itching of the eczema. For me, I was trying so hard to keep everything together and I felt like I was failing.'

Nick was also desperately worried about Michael. He'd had his eighteenth birthday six months before, and Nick became more and more concerned that, now no longer a minor, his son might be deported on his own. He came up with what he thought was a foolproof plan. He had a Russian friend, Pasha, who used to work for him and now lived in Vietnam. So, Michael should travel to Vietnam, apply for a working visa for Australia while he was there, then return on his new visa. Although he realised it would be a gamble, hopefully at least one of the family would then be lawful, and Michael would have a chance to get his life back on track. Michael liked the plan.

'I wanted to do the lawful thing,' he says. 'I thought, *Let's do right by the Australian Government; let's play by their rules.* I thought I'd have a holiday there for a month, then come back and everything would be back in my control, which would feel good. I was both excited and worried.'

Even better, if it all worked out well for Michael, then Anya could follow in six months' time, when she turned eighteen, and also end up back in Australia on a working visa.

With Anya, Nick drove Michael to Perth Airport on 27 August 2018 and they said a sad farewell. Nick tried to cheer up himself and Anya. 'I kept thinking, *This is going to be good for him*. He'd wasted too much time when he should have been out enjoying himself and doing boy stuff like I did when I was growing up. It was a *Go into the world, my son* kind of moment. I felt it would open his eyes to the world, be a brilliant experience and then he'd come back with a visa and everything would be great.'

Michael wasn't quite as optimistic about having a good time, but he was looking forward to getting away. 'I knew it would be only for a month, so it wouldn't be life-changing,' he says. 'But I was surprised Anya was so upset about saying goodbye. I kept saying to her that everything would be all right, I'd be back soon. What could possibly go wrong?'

So, Nick and Anya waved him goodbye and told him to phone as soon as he arrived in Vietnam so they'd know he was okay. It wasn't until they got back to the car park that Nick broke down. 'But that was all right,' he says. 'It was important to me that he didn't see me so upset, that he wouldn't worry.'

Ten hours later, Nick's phone rang. It was Michael. The good news was that he'd arrived safely; the bad news was that, as he was leaving Australia, immigration officials had examined his passport and told him, as he'd overstayed his visa, he wouldn't be allowed back into Australia for another three years.

# TWENTY-FOUR
# THE QUIET AUSTRALIAN

**MICHAEL HAD BEEN CONFUSED** when he was stopped at immigration.

'Did you realise you have a three-year ban?' the officer had asked him.

'No,' Michael replied. 'No, I didn't.'

'Well, do you have any money with you?' the officer continued.

Michael showed him his wallet, with around $1000 in Vietnamese dong inside. The man nodded.

'He had a funny look on his face,' Michael says. 'I didn't quite know what it was, but I realised later it was concern, like they couldn't quite work out what was happening, either. But it seemed crazy. Here I was, trying to do the right thing, leaving and then coming back in with a legitimate tourist visa, and I was being punished for it.'

When Michael walked out of the Tan Son Nhat International Airport in Ho Chi Minh City, he was met by Pasha, who drove him straight into the city. There, he was even more bewildered. Before leaving Bunbury, he'd watched a few movies about Vietnam to prepare himself. 'I had this picture in my head that I'd be in a tiny little village and going out into remote forests and jungles and be surrounded by unexploded bombs,' he says. 'But it was nothing like that. It was all hotels. I was glad, though. I didn't really feel like I wanted to be in forests.'

After a few days in Saigon, being amazed by the crowds, the traffic and the aggressive way people were driving, Michael was even more flummoxed. 'I thought, *What on earth am I doing here?*' he says. 'It was such a shock after being in the bush. But then I thought that this is the way people live here, so I have to be the same, driving on the footpaths and weaving through traffic like the Vietnamese. I had to adapt.'

Pasha had a house in the coastal resort city of Nha Trang. So, after a few days, the pair caught the bus there. A couple of days later, Michael checked into a $1-a-day dormitory and Pasha gave him a half-hour lesson on how to ride a hired 250cc bike. It was a baptism of fire as Michael had never even ridden a bicycle before, but he rose to the challenge.

While he tended to keep to himself, Michael found the Vietnamese extremely friendly and eager to practise their English with him, and that the groups of Russians in town, for whom that beach is a favoured tourist destination, were excited to find someone who knew their language. Pasha suggested he get a job teaching English to children, but Michael was reluctant, feeling unqualified. He soon found out, however, that even speaking English wasn't a requisite for the job; the language centres just seemed to want anyone who looked vaguely Anglo to entertain the kids. Fast running out of money, Michael relented and was given a job, but never really enjoyed it. 'After being in the bush for so long, I really didn't know how to interact with children,' he says. When his three-month visa was close to running out, he crossed the border into Cambodia in order to apply for a fresh three-month Vietnamese visa and then return.

Back in Australia, Nick was desperately working out not so much a Plan B, but more, he says, a Plan W, X or Y, having been, by then, through almost the entire alphabet. If Michael overstayed his second visa in Vietnam, Nick felt sure his son would be deported to Britain, where the threat of Russian retaliation most likely persisted.

'I didn't want to be there, looking over my shoulder all the time and worrying that something might happen when the kids were with me,' says Nick. 'The Salisbury poisoning case had been a big shock. Even if there was only a one per cent chance I'd get murdered, then I'd rather do something else. Percentages don't matter; the fact that there's even a chance is more important. So, the next realistic options were New Zealand or Canada. It sounds bizarre, but when you're running out of options, you've just got to keep going. You have to do something.'

With Anya's eighteenth birthday only a month and a half away, Nick put together his strategy. It involved leaving Anya safely with her best friend's parents in Bunbury and taking himself over to Vietnam to join Michael. Then they'd try to exit the country together, for New Zealand. Finally, Anya would follow them over from Australia.

It was an agonising decision. Nick knew he had to go to Vietnam to look after Michael but hated leaving Anya. The day he told her of the plan, they both tried to hold their emotions in check. 'We won't be separated for long,' he kept telling her. 'It'll probably be about three months, tops. Then we'll all be together again.'

Later, he describes it as the hardest decision he'd ever made. And the worst.

The pair had a final-farewell trip back to Broome, just for old times' sake, and stayed at the local campsite. The owner struck up a conversation with them one day, and Nick mentioned they'd once lived at Banana Well. At that, the man's eyes lit up.

'Did you know,' he said, nodding sagely, 'that a family of Russian spies stayed there for a few years once? The whole town is talking about it!'

Nick and Anya could barely keep a straight face. Later, on the jetty at Broome, they looked out over the water and laughed long and hard. It felt good after so many tears.

Nick finally booked a flight to Vietnam for 22 November 2018. As he packed, he marvelled at how, at the age of fifty, the entirety of his worldly possessions could fit into a single sports bag. He said goodbye to Anya, as cheerily as he could. She reassured him that she was fine with him leaving her to go to help Michael. As consolation, she'd be able to have a birthday party for her eighteenth after missing out on birthday parties for the past five years. She gave him her beloved MP3 player so he'd have music to listen to on the plane and when he was in Vietnam. He told her she should keep it, but she insisted. 'It's only going to be for three months,' she said. 'You can give it back to me then.'

He then gave her $500, which she tried to refuse. But this time, he insisted. They hugged and he climbed into his hire car to drive to the airport. When he looked around to wave for the last time, she could see tears in his eyes.

Nick actually cried all the way to the airport. But as he went through immigration, he took a deep breath, wondering if he'd be told he had a three-year ban on re-entering Australia, too. The official checked his passport, looked at the screen and frowned. Nick prepared himself.

'It says here you have an alert on you for the next fifty years,' the man said. 'Until 2069.'

Nick couldn't really comprehend what he was being told. Fifty years before he could come back into Australia? It seemed absolutely ridiculous. 'Thanks, mate,' he replied. There just didn't seem to be anything else to say.

Michael met Nick at the airport in Ho Chi Minh City and the pair caught up over a couple of beers, something they'd never done before. It felt like a rite of passage for them both. They then travelled to Nha Trang together, with Nick telling his son about his plan for New Zealand.

'It was great to see him, but he was super-stressed,' Michael says. 'He was worried about leaving Anya back in Australia and he was working so hard on trying to think of ways to get us all together somewhere safe. And then he'd been told he couldn't go back to Australia, so that was something big to process, too.'

Almost immediately, however, Nick learned that Anya wasn't coping with the absence of both her father and brother. She would contact Nick on Facebook Messenger and he would call her every day; sometimes they'd speak to each other up to six times a day. Nick would do his best to try to keep her calm and focused on the positives. But it didn't seem to be working. She continued having panic attacks and they were growing steadily worse. She'd also begun self-harming again.

'I was angry and upset and depressed all the time,' Anya says. 'I became so low, I was on the verge of suicide. I was crying and self-harming and then I thought that if those things didn't show how serious things were, then maybe I should stop eating. So, that's what I did.'

Anya's misery brought a fresh urgency to Nick and Michael's plan for getting out of Vietnam to somewhere safe where they could organise for Anya to join them, and as quickly as possible. Nick always kept half an eye on the Biloela family's case; their appeal against deportation had just been rejected by the Federal Court despite the family having a massive community campaign, Home To Bilo, behind them.

Having bought tickets on Vietnam Airlines to Auckland, he and Michael travelled back to Ho Chi Minh City and on to the airport. At the check-in counter, however, they struck a problem. The flight transited via Sydney and the Australian immigration authorities had blacklisted them, so they were suddenly being stopped from boarding the plane. 'We lost all our money on those two tickets, which was just sickening,' Nick says.

Michael was devastated, too. 'That was a real low point for me,' he says. 'I thought we were getting out of there, and then we were suddenly bounced back into the situation. It felt that every step we took was being thrown back at us, no matter what it was.'

They returned to Nha Trang to work out what to do next. It all seemed suddenly so hopeless, especially with Anya apparently in ever more desperate straits back in Bunbury. Then Nick had another idea. On 14 January 2019, he emailed the American journalist Michael Weiss, to whom he'd leaked those Shuvalov papers three years before. When they'd originally talked, Weiss had raised the possibility that the family might be able to gain refugee status in the USA, so Nick asked him now if there was anything he could possibly do to help. Weiss said maybe there was something he could do. After all, he had something like 123,000 followers to call on in times of need. Nick thanked him profusely.

Two days later, Nick and Michael were sitting on a small Vietnamese bus on the way to their local V3 Café when Michael suddenly paled.

'Dad, you'd better have a look at this,' he whispered, and showed him the screen of his phone.

Nick took it and stared. It had Nick's name on it, along with a tweet from Weiss saying, *A former source of mine, who passed along secret documents about Russia's Deputy Prime Minister Igor Shuvalov's unexplained wealth and expenditures, is facing, along with his family, deportation from Australia. Here's the story he was a source for: https://t.co/NJWA6HRBl7 — Michael Weiss (@michaeldweiss) 16 January 2019*

Nick could hardly believe his eyes. Weiss had named him in a tweet as the source of all the leaked documents about Shuvalov! And as he watched, the screen lit up with comments and retweets. Within hours, there had been hundreds of responses to the tweet; Nick couldn't keep up. Michael read a number of them out and, trying to buoy his father, pointed out that 99 per cent of them were positive about Nick's actions, and supportive of the family. 'But we were so shocked that my name had been exposed,' says Nick. 'It gave us immediate attention worldwide, but it probably wasn't really the kind of attention we'd been after.'

Weiss emailed Nick to say there was now huge media interest in his story, but Nick couldn't really see how that would help. But Weiss suggested he email a man named Bill Browder for advice and assistance. Nick used his phone to research him. Browder was an

American-born British financier whose company was at one time the biggest foreign-portfolio investor in Russia. When he fell out of favour with the Russians, and they raided his company, he commissioned tax expert Sergei Magnitsky to investigate. Magnitsky was imprisoned by the regime and died in prison. Browder later persuaded President Obama to pass a law, called the Magnitsky Act, to punish Russians who abused human rights. In 2015, he'd written a bestselling book about his time in Russia, *Red Notice: A True Story of High Finance, Murder, and One Man's Fight for Justice*. Nick emailed him to ask for help, and immediately received a reply. The email said he was in grave danger being in Vietnam, a country that was a close friend of Russia's. 'You need to get out of Vietnam NOW!' it read.

Nick swallowed hard. It was just like the warning he'd received from Weiss back in 2014 to disappear in Australia when his original article about Shuvalov came out. 'Now I knew we were definitely in the shit,' he says. 'Michael and I started really panicking. We changed hotels every day, and we were convinced, every day, that the police would come and get us. Bill Browder said he knew someone else had been detained at the airport, so we should be very, very careful. It made us determined to get out as quickly as we could. Even worse, we could see a Chinese website that was all in Mandarin, except for two words in English right in the middle: Nicholas Stride. My name stood out like a sore thumb. And then our photo appeared on it. I thought, *Oh, my God, this is mental.* Then three Russian sites started carrying the story, with my name. So, I said to Michael, "That's it. Even if we weren't in the shit before, we certainly are up to our necks in it now." Just when you think things can't get worse, they do.'

Michael took his point, realising that it wasn't such a great idea to be in a country that's a socialist republic with a one-party system led by the Communist Party when you were nervous of retaliations from Russia. 'It would be very easy in such an authoritarian country for the police to arrest you and send you back to Russia,' Michael says. 'Every time I went out, I started looking for police officers and every night, I'd be ready for the door to be kicked open and police to come in.'

Meanwhile, the flood of tweets continued, with people suggesting Nick flee to New Zealand, the US, Canada or even to Australia. New Zealanders joined in, saying Nick should contact their immigration minister, Iain Lees-Galloway; Australian sympathisers also suggested tactics. At the same time, Browder suggested Nick and Michael should agree to do interviews with any media who asked.

Nick ended up doing one story with Channel 7 in Australia, on a live cross via Skype, and another with *The Guardian Australia* online, which appeared under the headline, *British man and family plead for asylum after hiding in Australia in fear of Russian threats.* ABC TV contacted Anya in Bunbury and conducted an interview with her, too, and then put the story online as: *Russian whistleblower's teenage daughter comes forward after 9-year outback exile.*

The media was overwhelmingly sympathetic, and journalists had apparently gone to the Immigration Department for a reaction, but always received the same one: 'The Department does not comment on individual cases or matters which are before the court.'

Nick also called the immigration department in New Zealand and asked if he could apply for refugee status. The person he spoke to wasn't so helpful, though, armed with that much-hated response: the office couldn't comment on individual cases.

Close to the end of his tether, Nick decided they should just get on a plane to New Zealand and try to sort it all out when they got there. Michael searched through Chinese websites looking for the cheapest flights available. He came up with one on VietJet from Ho Chi Minh to Taipei in Taiwan. From there, they could catch a Chinese airline flight to Auckland. They bought two tickets with almost the last of their money.

On 5 February 2019, their hearts pounding, they returned to the airport, made it through Vietnamese immigration without a hitch and landed in Taipei three and a half hours later. The next day was Michael's birthday, but while Nick wanted to buy him a present and have a few drinks with him to celebrate, Michael flatly refused. 'I know he wanted to make the day a good time, but we had to save all the money we could,' Michael says. 'I felt if we could save one cent, I was saving it.'

Six days later, they boarded a flight to Auckland. It was an exciting moment but heavy with anxiety. They'd still have the hurdle of getting through immigration in New Zealand, knowing they'd probably both have alerts attached to their names.

# TWENTY-FIVE
# HITTING ROCK BOTTOM

WHEN THE PAIR LANDED in Auckland on Monday 11 February 2019, they approached the automated immigration zone with trepidation. Nick went first on the thumbprint machine that would either approve him, and swing the gates open, or deny him entry. He put his thumb down and the machine's screen flashed up with a cross. His heart sank. He tried again, with the same result. He was just beginning to panic when an official came over.

'Oh,' he said casually, 'this machine always does that. Here you go, I'll swipe you in.' He did exactly the same for Michael.

The pair emerged into a warm, clear day in New Zealand's biggest city. But as the reality of their situation hit home, their elation began to ebb. They now had just $130 left to their names, and a bus ticket to the city centre alone cost $30. So, they began to walk.

'We noticed an estuary in the distance and for some reason we decided to walk there,' says Nick. 'It was a bit mad as this was a big city, but we wanted to see the estuary and wondered if we could

257

fish there. We were walking through the grass and both looking down at our feet until suddenly we realised we didn't have to – this was a country without snakes or venomous spiders or, in fact, anything that could kill you. We could just walk through the grass and be safe. It all felt very strange.'

By the time they finally reached the city, Nick had made up his mind: it was time for both of them to give up. They were virtually broke, they knew no one there and had no idea what their next step should be.

'Let's go to the British Consulate,' Nick suggested to Michael. 'We'll tell them what's happened to us, and just put our lives in their hands. It's the only option we've got now.'

The pair went into the consulate office the next morning and explained their situation, handing over a series of documents and pointing to all the media stories that had appeared on them for back-up. The official listened quietly and took detailed notes. Finally, he looked back up. 'Thank you,' he said. 'Now we'll have to refer this back to London.'

Nick and Michael both tried to hide their disappointment as they went back out into the city. Unable to afford anywhere to stay, they slept in parks or on the streets, and were living on cheap bread and cheese from the supermarkets with the occasional $1 hot chocolate from McDonald's. 'They were cheaper than water,' Michael says. Though they'd faced plenty of low points before, Nick felt they'd finally hit rock bottom.

Two days later, they returned to the British Consulate. This time, the same official had an answer for them. He said he couldn't help, but if they wanted him to contact a family member to buy tickets for them back to the UK, he could arrange the call.

Nick was outraged. 'That's not what we're asking for,' he exploded. 'You've seen the paperwork. You've read the stories. I'm asking the British Government for protection.'

The man looked nonplussed. 'Okay,' he said. 'I need to talk to someone else. I'll email you. No need to come in again.'

Outside the consulate, Nick felt close to giving up entirely. But that wasn't an option. Michael and Anya, who was still having an horrendous time back in Australia, were depending on him.

'We'd been sleeping rough, but I said to Michael that we weren't doing that anymore,' Nick says. 'We couldn't. We were there with all the down-and-outs and drunks and homeless people in Auckland, and I said I didn't care what happened to us, but we weren't doing that any longer.'

Michael had been researching New Zealand on his phone and said he'd found that Christchurch, the country's third-largest city behind Auckland and the capital Wellington, and the largest on the South Island, offered the best chance for work and the cheapest housing. Nick listened carefully.

'Right,' he said. 'Let's go to Christchurch. We'll just start walking there. Something will happen. Somewhere along the line we'll meet someone or we could do some work on a farm or something. I'm just not staying in Auckland, living on the streets.' Shades of that old family motto again: We always find a way.

The idea of walking the 1070 kilometres from Auckland to Christchurch wasn't enormously appealing to Michael. 'But I thought, *Well, I suppose it could make the news and then someone might offer us a job*,' he says. 'Everything was so stressful, though, I just wanted it to be over.'

Before they set off, Nick tried one last thing: putting an ad on social media saying that two people had landed in New Zealand in a desperate situation; they were looking for work and willing to do anything. A few negative comments came back, like, 'Go back home! There's not enough work for us already here!' But then they had a call from a Tongan man named Kova, who asked about their work experience and then said they could start on his site the next day. What's more, when he heard they had nowhere to stay, he booked them into a local backpackers hostel and paid for their lodging, saying he'd take it out of their wages later, and then shouted them both a McDonald's meal. It felt like manna from heaven.

They started work the next day, joining Kova's team to build timber-framed houses in the South Auckland suburb of Manurewa. Nick worked as a carpenter and Michael was a hammer hand. Everyone in the team worked ten-hour days, so they were, at last, making good money. Their workmates were friendly, too, and the well-built Tongans loved challenging their new workmates to weight-lifting contests. Nick and Michael didn't stand a chance. After the first few days, recognising they were proving such good workers, Kova checked them out of the hostel and gave them a spare room in his house.

Shortly afterwards, an email came through from the British Consulate. It said that they couldn't help. 'For us, that was a huge shock,' Nick says. 'They totally turned their back on us. So, we decided to go and talk to New Zealand immigration, tell them what had happened and see what they said. And that was the biggest shock of all.'

Nick and Michael walked into the offices of Immigration New Zealand on Thursday 14 February 2019 to apply for refugee status or protection, and their reception couldn't have been more differ-ent from the one they'd been given in Australia. As soon as Nick had told his story, they were concerned and sympathetic. They gave him a list of lawyers he could choose from, with the New Zealand system providing free government-funded legal assistance for most stages of the visa application process. They also made sure that he and Michael had somewhere to live. They said they were, in this case, prepared to overlook the fact that the pair had been working illegally, acknowledging they needed money to live.

'It was a breath of fresh air,' Nick says. 'People were actually listening to us! And it made a huge difference having a lawyer for the first time, and the one we chose was so smart and kind and clever. It felt like people were understanding what we'd been through in the last twelve years. They even sympathised with my fear of going back to Britain. They got it all straight away. It wasn't like immigration officers talking to us; it was like the Red Cross!'

As the process of applying to stay in New Zealand got underway, Nick's calls to Anya became even more frequent. She was still having a terrible time back in Australia, now suffering from anorexia as well as anxiety and depression. He'd been away for over two and a half months, and she was finding it increasingly hard to believe they'd be together again within that promised three months.

But Nick shared with her every step they were taking with Immigration New Zealand and kept saying that it now wouldn't be long. They just had to wait, he reassured her, for decisions on their applications and then hopefully their visas and permanent residen-cies would follow.

Then, as soon as he had enough money saved from his new job, he sent her over the fare for a flight to Auckland.

The next day when he talked to her, she sounded much brighter. She said she was on her way to buy a plane ticket. She told him she was due to arrive in three days' time, and he and Michael were both thrilled, and enormously relieved.

But on the morning she was due to arrive, they were about to head out to the airport when they received a phone call from Anya. She was in tears. She'd been about to board her plane when immigration officials stopped her.

# TWENTY-SIX
# ONLY THE LONELY

BACK IN BUNBURY, Anya was doing it tough. Without her dad and brother, and estranged from her mother, she wasn't coping. She'd had that longed-for eighteenth birthday party on 2 January 2019 but, in the event, hadn't enjoyed it at all. Sick with worry about Nick and Michael and regretting not accompanying her father to Vietnam so the trio could be reunited and work out their futures together, she was completely overwhelmed by feelings of regret and guilt.

'My birthday came around and I almost drank myself to death,' Anya says. 'It was the first time I'd ever drunk alcohol . . . and the last. I didn't know what I was doing. I was just too young. I didn't understand anything. Dad thinks it's his fault, that he should never have gone and left me, but it wasn't. We just did what we thought was right. We thought we'd be separated for three months. We didn't know it would end up [being] much, much longer.'

Anya started off living at different friends' places. but she was so sad and depressed, she knows she was hard to be around. Some of

263

those friends didn't really want her there in their homes, she believes, and often she moved so as not to outstay her welcome. One time, she ended up taking a room in the house of a friend's uncle but was then petrified living there with him, alone. 'I was so scared,' she says. At that point, a friend's concerned mum took her in, and gave her the caravan in their backyard.

'I told them it would just be for three months,' Anya says. 'But I lied. I knew by then that it was going to be longer. But I was frightened, and I didn't want to move again. Dad couldn't do anything. He was stuck. And months were passing and everything was going horribly wrong. I didn't really trust anyone because everyone was either leaving me, or I had to leave them. I became angry and difficult to live with.'

Angie, who provided her with the caravan and encouraged her to feel a part of the family, felt the young girl had touched her heart. 'Anya was very up and down and some days she really struggled with diet and her mental health,' Angie says. 'We sought professional help for her with that. She talked about death and there were a few panicked moments when we knew she wanted to do herself in. I just felt God had put her on our doorstep to help her and a lot of prayers were going up during that time.

'She was a lovely girl, with a very kind heart, and it was easy to see that she'd been through a lot of trauma. To be separated from her family was very hard for her. It was terribly, terribly sad, and my heart went out to her. We just tried to do what we could to help.'

When Anya received the call from her dad that they'd applied for refugee status in New Zealand, and it looked as if, in time, it might be successful, she momentarily emerged from the blackness. Nick sent her over the money for a plane ticket and she bought one and made all the arrangements to leave. She farewelled the family and all her friends in Bunbury and set off for the airport.

Her joy, however, was short-lived. At the airport's check-in counter, airline staff told her New Zealand wasn't prepared to let her in. She could barely believe it. In floods of tears, she called her dad to give him the news.

He immediately contacted his immigration lawyer, who confirmed the bad news. The lawyer told him that, when someone claims asylum, family members with the same name are normally not allowed to enter the country. There'd been an alert that had been triggered when she'd tried to check in.

Nick called his daughter back and gently explained the situation. 'I'm so sorry, Anya,' he said, his heart breaking as he heard her sobbing on the other end of the line. 'That's all my fault. I didn't know. But I promise you, I promise, it won't be too long before you can come over here, and we'll all be together again.'

That journey back to Bunbury was one of the most miserable Anya had ever undertaken in her life.

'Everything hit me then,' she says. 'And being there on my own stretched from three months to more and more and then to years.'

Depressed, suffering panic attacks, self-harming, battling an eating disorder and suicidal, Anya ended up in the local hospital. Then staff transferred her to its psychiatric ward, where she spent almost a month.

'I remember when I was in the ward, I pleaded with them not to send me home,' she says. 'I liked it there. But they said I couldn't stay longer, and they sent me to a holiday house for troubled people for two weeks. Then they discharged me, and things got even worse.

'Every second of the day I felt like I was wearing a dark cloak and I saw nothing but darkness. I didn't care if I hurt anyone's feelings because all I wanted to do was to die. I didn't care if anything happened to me. I would lie on the floor listening to the loudest music I could and I felt no hope. I felt dead inside and living felt so, so heavy. I wanted to commit suicide, but I was scared. I used to do voluntary work at a charity clothing shop, and one woman there took me under her wing. She said later that I was on death's door at the time, and I think she was right. I was completely broken. I was finished. I'd call Dad a lot and cry on the phone to him, and he'd cry too. It almost broke my heart to hear him crying. I told him how I felt, and he said he sometimes felt the same way.'

Family friend Steve Delane could see how much Anya was struggling. 'I think she found it very hard when Nick and Michael went overseas,' he says. 'She was a strong, independent young lady; she wouldn't have survived everything she has without being like that. It would have been so hard to go through all that at such a young age.'

Often, Anya was so upset when she called her father that it would take him fifteen minutes to calm her down enough that she could talk, she'd be hyperventilating so badly. He'd frequently be so agonisingly worried after those calls that, on many occasions, he came close to asking the police to check up on her. 'If I couldn't get hold of her I would panic and keep calling until she answered,' he says. 'A few times, she'd just be having a shower and pick up her phone to see thirty missed calls. She was just wasting away physically and emotionally. Every day, I waited for a call to say she had ended her life.'

It was so difficult for Anya, being by herself back in Australia, Michael says. 'I felt for her. I really did. She was having so many difficulties and we were far away and there was nothing we could do. We'd talk to her, but she always sounded so down.'

She'd suffered before with depression, back on The Beach, but there, the daily battle to survive had kept her too busy to dwell on her circumstances. Now, she had too little to do, so spent long periods curled up on the floor or on the couch, alone in the caravan. It was always worse when her friends got together with their families and invited her along – somehow seeing them all enjoying one another's company, or at Christmas time, it made her miss her dad and brother's company even more keenly.

Finally, Anya was put on a course of antidepressants, which she feels may well have saved her life. Almost miraculously, much of that heaviness dissipated.

All through that time, however, never once did Anya suggest she and her dad FaceTime each other or talk on Zoom, where they'd be able to see each other's faces. Nor did Nick ever float the idea. Despite speaking to each other every single day, and often multiple times a day, they both knew that looking at each other could prove unbearable.

Then, one day, a contact of Nick's who'd spoken to him on Zoom asked if they could talk again, but this time include Anya on the call. Nick hesitated, then rang Anya and asked her. She wasn't keen.

'But we agreed and, five minutes before the call, I thought we should check each other out on the video first,' Nick says. 'So, we turned it on and we'd both done exactly the same thing: we'd positioned the cameras so we could only see the top of each other's heads. It was incredible, and we cracked up laughing. And then we moved the cameras so we could see each other. It was very hard, but that moment had made it so special. After that, we started calling each other on video.'

Anya remembers that day well. 'He cried when he saw me,' she says. 'I guess I probably looked a bit pale and thin. But he said how much he loved me and missed me, so we both ended up crying all over again.'

# TWENTY-SEVEN
# THE KINDNESS OF STRANGERS

NICK HAD BEEN PRIMED by his new lawyer for the hearing about to take place in Auckland to determine whether he and Michael would be allowed to stay as refugees in New Zealand. By the time he walked into the small courtroom, he felt he'd never been more ready in his life to plead his case. But then the presiding member of the Immigration and Protection Tribunal, instead of starting on her opening statement, said something completely unexpected.

'How's Anya?' she asked.

Nick looked at her in surprise. And then he completely broke down. 'You know, all the things she could have said, and all the questions she was likely to ask – about my background, what had led us to this point, what we'd done in Australia – and yet she asked about Anya. That simple gesture of kindness completely threw me.

'She seemed so sympathetic, too. She said she understood how difficult our situation was but that she wanted to reassure me that they were going to sort out everything in the fairest way possible. They weren't there to persecute us.'

It had been a tough nineteen months since he and Michael had first walked into the Auckland offices of Immigration New Zealand. There were many times when they felt all was lost, and they might never be given permission to stay. They were also terrified about what Anya might do, back in Western Australia. She'd already tried to commit suicide once, and Nick was desperate to bring her to New Zealand to join them. This hearing, on 22 September 2020, held the key to all their futures.

It seemed to go well, but then Nick and Michael could never really tell. As they left the courtroom that day to drive back down to their new home in Christchurch, they could only hope against hope that they might be close to the end of their quest. They'd spent three months working with Kova in Auckland but had both longed to go somewhere quieter, away from the city. At first, they tried Minginui, a small town in the Bay of Plenty Region, 350 kilometres south of Auckland. Along the way, they visited the rolling green hills and black sand beaches of Waikato, Tauranga, with its magnificent Mount Maunganui and Rotorua's steaming hot springs, bubbling mud pools and geysers. 'It was great to see a bit of New Zealand and it was so different to Australia,' says Michael, now twenty. 'But while Minginui was nice, there wasn't much work there, so after a couple of months, we decided to try Christchurch instead.'

They then drove another 900 kilometres south, via Napier, Hastings and Palmerston North to Wellington, and caught the ferry to the South Island. From there, they passed via Picton, Blenheim and Kaikoura, stopping finally in Christchurch. It was a place that, as Michael had predicted, suited them both. Quiet, picturesque and the perfect base to explore the Southern Alps and Canterbury Plains, it also offered plenty of construction work.

It was there, too, that Nick and Luda's divorce finally came through. It felt like a good place to heal.

Every day, Nick and Michael called Anya, now nineteen, to tell her about their surroundings and everything new they were seeing. Nick would show her photos over Facebook and Michael would play video games with her. They were both doing their best to try to distract her. In turn, she repeated that there was an interesting rumour going around Bunbury: that they'd apparently had Russian spies living in their midst. It was an interesting twist on the media stories everybody had seen on TV and read in the press about the family. Nick and Michael laughed, but redoubled their efforts to convince her that it hopefully wouldn't be long before they'd be granted New Zealand visas, and then they could bring her over the Tasman to join them.

There were events going on in the world that seemed to make it even more urgent that they succeed in being able to stay in New Zealand, too. In Australia, the Nadesalingam family from Biloela, who'd been fighting their own deportation order, had lost their final appeal in the High Court and were put on a plane – only for it to be sensationally forced to land in Darwin when a last-minute legal injunction was granted. Then, they'd been taken back to detention on Christmas Island.

Meanwhile, in Russia, prominent opposition figure Alexei Navalny fell ill on a flight between the Siberian city of Tomsk and Moscow and, after an emergency landing in the city of Omsk, was put into an induced coma. Two days later, he was evacuated to Germany as it was revealed that he'd been poisoned with Novichok, with Putin accused of being behind the attack. It had come only two months after fellow Novichok victims Sergei Skripal and his daughter Yulia were reported to be living in hiding under assumed names in New Zealand.

Finally, on 23 March 2021, the news came that everyone had been waiting for: the tribunal had ruled that Nick and Michael could stay. Nick had been classified as a protected person within the meaning of the Convention Against Torture, while Michael was a refugee under the meaning of the Refugee Convention. Thrilled, Nick phoned Anya. 'It won't be long now,' he told his daughter. 'It can't be.'

It had been two and half years since he'd left his daughter, but he felt confident the end was now in sight. But time dragged on and it felt they were getting no closer to securing a visa for Anya. The world changed around them – COVID-19 came and subsided; Russia invaded Ukraine – but Nick's family were standing still. He grew desperate. His lawyer assured him he was trying to expedite the process, but it was proving to be excruciatingly slow. Someone even said it could be another eighteen months, which would extend their separation to four years, which Nick felt sure Anya wouldn't be able to endure. Her self-harming, depression and eating disorder were all potential threats to her life.

Eventually, he came up with his Plan Z. He would rent a second-hand yacht and sail to Australia via Norfolk Island and Lord Howe Island, and they would pick up Anya from a deserted beach somewhere on the east coast.

They knew it would be a treacherous voyage, with the Tasman Sea notorious as one of the roughest waterbodies on earth. Winds and waves were turbulent for most of the year, particularly between April and October when they'd be sailing. There was a high risk the expedition would fail.

'But we were desperate,' Nick says. 'We were sure we were going to lose Anya. We knew the Tasman was one of the most dangerous stretches of water on the planet, but we felt we had no other option. We had to take the chance. This had to end. Anya would not die alone. And if it ended in my death out there on the water, then so be it. At least I'd tried. I told Michael that it was something I had to do alone because it was so risky, but he would have none of it. He insisted he'd come with me. We both felt that no person, no law or no immigration department was going to stop our family getting back together. It was another life-threatening dilemma, but one we felt we had to undertake. We started working on the route.'

In the weeks spent planning and preparing, Nick put a FOI application into the New Zealand system and found the email addresses of the people at the top of the immigration hierarchy. He then emailed them all, saying he and Michael had been allowed to stay, so there was no reason Anya shouldn't be allowed to join them, particularly as she was at such high risk. Nick decided that, if no one came back to him, or someone came back to say it was impossible to bring her over, that would be their cue to depart. But the very next day, he received a phone call from an immigration officer. 'Hold tight,' she said. 'We're on the case. We're going to fast-track Anya's application.'

The world suddenly seemed a kinder place. Back in Australia, the Biloela family had a Ministerial Intervention and were told they could finally return home. Nick looked on enviously.

And while it took six weeks, on 22 July 2022, Nick finally received the call he'd been dreaming of for so long, informing him that he and Michael, twenty-two, had been granted permanent-residence visas, while twenty-one-year-old Anya had been included as a dependent daughter on Nick's visa. He was overjoyed.

'He called me up and there was a pause, and I just knew what he was going to say,' Anya recounts. 'He said, "We did it!" And I just said, "Great!" It was an amazing moment, but I didn't cry. I think I'd been ready for that moment for so long. There was no need to cry anymore. Nothing mattered. Everything would be okay now.'

Not quite everything was, however. In Anya's three and a half years alone in Australia, she'd ended up moving home a total of nine times. The family she was now staying with all came down with COVID two days before she was due to leave. She fretted that she'd picked it up, but fortunately, she was all clear. Walking through the departure gates in Perth, ready for her flight to Sydney, she looked back at the last family who'd taken her in, waved, smiled and then burst into tears.

For the entire four and a bit hours of the flight, she was inconsolable. After so many months of not eating properly, she'd been too weak to lift her hand luggage up into the overhead lockers, so someone had done it for her. Then everyone kept asking if she was all right. 'I think I was just crying out all the hardship and the memories of the last twelve years,' Anya says.

She had to spend the night in Sydney and, as soon as she reached the hotel, she collapsed on the bed and slept for a solid fourteen hours. When she woke, to dozens of missed calls from her dad, panicking because he hadn't heard from her, she caught a bus to Bondi Beach just to gaze at the beach and the ocean beyond. Somewhere in the distance would be New Zealand, set to be her new home. When she headed back to the airport, she became hopelessly lost, and then a wheel on her bag broke, so she was hauling it around after her. Finally, she made it back, and, predictably, was stopped at immigration.

'Why did you overstay your visa?' an officer asked her.

'It's a long story,' she replied.

'But do you now know you have a three-year ban?'

'Yes,' Anya said, with a smile. 'I know. Okay, thank you.'

She then boarded the plane just before 9pm and flew for three hours direct to Christchurch. Nick and Michael were taking no risks. If she had trouble with New Zealand customs, they wanted to be right there for her. In the air, Anya could barely contain her excitement.

Because of the time difference, her plane arrived in the pitch dark at 2am on Friday 29 July 2022. She went straight through immigration but, after she picked up her bag from the luggage carousel, she stood for a few minutes at the doors leading out into the arrivals hall. She wanted to prepare herself.

'I'd daydreamed about this moment for so long, and imagined breaking into a run and just hugging Dad and Michael,' she says. 'But then I went through and saw them, and I hadn't seen them for so long, I just wanted to look and take it all in. Time slowed down and all the background noise ceased.'

She stood still, drinking in the sight of them. Nick was suddenly alarmed. 'I thought, *Maybe she doesn't remember me*,' he says. '*Maybe she thinks I've grown old*. She just looked at us.'

Michael felt suddenly awkward in the presence of his sister. They'd been talking on the phone for so long, it felt strange that now here she was suddenly, in the flesh.

Then they all fell into one another's arms and hugged and hugged as if they would never stop.

'Everyone was happy,' Anya says. 'We were quiet and just relieved and happy and grateful. It was so peaceful.'

And then the little trio went back to their house in Christchurch for Anya to open all the Christmas presents her dad and brother had bought for her over the past three years apart. Among them was a special one: her best-friend-to-be, a little Kelpie puppy Nick had just bought to help her adjust to her new life. He'd named her Molly.

'Our family was finally all together again,' Nick says, wiping the tears from his eyes. 'And now . . . and now . . . we are never letting go.'

# TWENTY-EIGHT
# NO REGRETS

THEY'RE A FAMILY LIVING quietly somewhere in the middle of New Zealand's North Island and, to the casual observer, look the picture of normality.

The man and woman are obviously devoted to each other, smiling and nodding in deep conversation, while the handsome young man – obviously the son – taps on his computer, and the daughter bends over a piece of jewellery she's carefully crafting, her long auburn hair falling over her face.

But this is Nick Stride today, with Michael and Anya, and Michael's new partner Mila, all absorbed in the task of building a new life for themselves. It hasn't been easy after living through such torrid times over the past eighteen years but, gradually, they're getting there.

'We're in a good place,' says Nick, now fifty-five. 'This is what I've been hoping for since, really, the kids were born: a good, happy home in a safe part of the world where they can live peacefully and hopefully realise their own dreams. It's been a long time coming but at last we've made it.

'We've had some good times, and some terrible times, but I don't really have any regrets. I could have done better, I know, but I always did what I thought was best for all of us at the time. There's no point in having regrets. Everything we've lived through has made us who we are today. And now, at last, it really does feel like it's happy ever after.'

Of course, not everything is perfect. While Nick feels privileged to have travelled to areas of Australia that had probably barely seen other human life before, he still dreams one day of going back to visit all the friends he made, and to see once more all the places that played such a significant role in his life's journey.

Michael, now twenty-three, feels the same. 'I like New Zealand, don't get me wrong,' he says. 'The government has been very, very good to us, and I will always be grateful. It's a great country. But I have to be honest, it just doesn't feel like home. Even though I was born in England, I've lived most of my life in Australia, and I still think of myself as Australian. Of course, I'm glad that we're here in New Zealand, but Australia is the country that will always feel like home to me.'

Anya, twenty-two, also says she's happy to be in New Zealand, but still gets homesick for Australia. 'I think my heart belongs to Australia, and it always will,' she says. 'I adore it so much. I guess it's just home to me.'

The children's mother, Nick's ex-wife Luda, stayed on in Australia hoping to win protection via a number of lawyer-submitted applications for Ministerial Intervention. She and Nick remain estranged, and she is no longer in contact with Michael or Anya. She is still hoping to be allowed to remain in Western Australia.

When Anya's three-year ban for overstaying their visas comes to an end, she'll be able to reapply for a Visitor visa to cross the Tasman for holidays, and Michael has already managed to be approved for one of these. Nick, however, is less sure about being allowed back in. That 50-year watch on his international comings and goings, with his fingerprints shared between the countries of the Five Eyes intelligence alliance – Australia, New Zealand, the UK, the USA and Canada – means a warning is still triggered every time he applies for a visa, and, so far, all his applications have been refused. 'That will last much longer than me!' Nick laughs.

In addition, he's classified red and 'sensitive' on the Movement Alert List, a computer database that's administered by Australia's Department of Home Affairs and which notifies immigration officials whenever he might try to enter Australia.

Family friend Steve Delane, back in Bunbury, is sympathetic. 'I do miss them,' he says. 'It would be great, one day, to see them living back here. I have a lot of admiration for Nick and the way he looked after his family and how resilient and resourceful he had to be to handle all that. They are all wonderful people, always ready to help others. I do hope everything continues to work out for them.'

Looking back over their difficulties, and in a bid to work out what went wrong, Nick applied for all his immigration records from the department under FOI provisions. He received around 8000 documents. Among them was a handwritten note 'from London', presumably in reply to an Australian immigration department's letter to the British authorities about Nick and the family, warning

Australia to be wary; Nick's case had the potential to trigger media interest.

Today, the Department of Home Affairs will shed little light on the whole affair. A department spokesperson said, 'The Department does not comment on individual cases due to privacy obligations. Australia provides protection consistent with its international obligations. The criteria for a protection visa, and the relevant tests, are set out in the statutory protection framework provisions of Australia's Migration Act 1958 (the Act) and Migration Regulations 1994. Each case is assessed on its merits, taking into account the individual circumstances of the case and the most current and relevant country of origin information.'

In addition, said the spokesperson, 'Australia does not return individuals to situations where they face persecution or a real risk of torture, cruel, inhuman or degrading treatment or punishment, arbitrary deprivation of life or the application of the death penalty.'

Yet Hannah Dickinson, principal solicitor, Human Rights Program at the Asylum Seeker Resource Centre, says the process potential refugees and asylum seekers have to go through in Australia can take an unacceptably long time, and puts huge pressure on the applicants. They face significant barriers at the same time as they are forced to live with the daily fear of being sent back to the situation they fear most, where they'll be exposed to torture, violence or loss of liberty – sometimes at best.

'The sadness and injustice of the stories we see is unrivalled,' Dickinson says. 'The Australian system is unnecessarily complex. With 2700-plus pages of laws and regulations, it's totally opaque and difficult to engage with, and the strict deadlines and rules mean missteps can cause people to lose their rights, including to review.

There's no legal representation in many cases, or entitlement to advice, but people with legal support are dramatically more likely to succeed because support to navigate this system is essential. That shouldn't be the case.

'Waiting years for an answer, with restrictions on the ability to work, study or receive medical help or governmental support and often having faced severe trauma, we see people become desperate and hopeless, with a major deterioration in their health. It can be very overwhelming to live with. And we also know that, due to defects in the system, decisions are being made that are wrong, so people who are entitled to refugee status are being forced to return to situations where they face serious harm. That's something Australia needs to take very seriously.'

Certainly, one of Nick's main hurdles was not receiving a lawyer to help guide the family through the process of applying for refugee status, and then not having one to perhaps organise to reapply through the broader grounds of the complementary protection provisions that came into effect in 2012.

Leading Australian immigration lawyer Nilesh Nandan advises that, generally, no one is permitted to make a second protection-visa application inside Australia after an earlier protection claim is refused – except on those grounds. 'Nick had a window in which he could have started the process again,' he says. 'And he would have stood a much greater chance of success, and then avoided everything that came after.'

Indeed, one of Nandan's own protection-visa clients did exactly this. His client, 'DAO16', the pseudonym given to an Indian Sikh man, claimed he would be at risk of significant harm, on account of his homosexuality, were he to be returned to his home country.

Before 2012, he was initially turned down, but he was able to reapply under the new provisions. The Full Court of the Federal Court quashed a decision made by a second Tribunal (ordering the Minister pay legal costs) and after a third tribunal considered the man's claims, it confirmed that the man was in fact owed protection obligations by Australia, under the new provisions.

Delane believes it made it harder for Nick and his children being from the UK. 'I think it meant they automatically got a "privilege" tag,' he says. 'People looked at them and thought they'd be okay, they didn't look like the kind of refugees we're used to seeing from ethnic backgrounds like Sri Lanka or Malaysia or Afghanistan. So people wouldn't automatically have the same kind of compassion for them. But they were *political* refugees . . . which was so different.'

From the successful community campaign to win the Biloela family the right to stay in Australia, one of the organisers, mental health social worker Angela Fredericks, muses on the government policies that made it so difficult both for her friends and, at the same time, for Nick and his family.

'I think it goes all the way back to the White Australia policy and then more recent governments doing such a great job of turning people coming to Australia into "others" who were different to us and represented danger and a threat to our lifestyle,' she says. 'The Biloela family and Nick and his family should have been seen as simply other human beings, just like us, who were looking for safety and needed our help. But instead of a protective response, it became a threat response. I think since 9/11, in 2001, it's been a particularly dark time, with this idea of protectionism being brought back to our borders. In the twenty years since then, it was all about protecting ourselves, rather than helping others.

'The other important thing is that our policies are so sweeping. They don't try to take individual circumstances into account. In the case of the Biloela family, they said Sri Lanka is safe – but of course it is for some people, but not for others. In the same way, they would have seen Britain as safe for Nick, when it obviously wasn't in his case. But our policies lump everyone together rather than looking at individual cases.'

Associate Professor Maria O'Sullivan of the Deakin Law School says what Nick's case does exemplify is that the Ministerial discretion to give a visa on humanitarian grounds is highly subjective.

'I am not sure why the Ministerial discretion power was not granted here,' she says. 'The test is "exceptional circumstances", but the fact that it was not in this case does say a lot about the gaps in our refugee legal regime in Australia. That is, perhaps there should be a visa class for this type of case, or at least some sort of widening of the criteria.'

To add to the complexities, from December 2007 to December 2020, Australia has had no fewer than ten different immigration ministers.

Nick sees the issues with Russia as also partly to blame. The US journalist Michael Weiss had made serious allegations against a very powerful politician and businessman in Russia, using some of the documents Nick had provided. Politically, however, having an Australian government backing Nick at that time might have triggered repercussions from Russia.

'The Russians have business deals all over the world, and no government wants to upset them,' Nick says. 'If Australia had granted us protection, they might have seen it as saying that some of Weiss's allegations were valid, so it was easier to dump on us, rather than do the right thing. They admitted we were in danger, but then they refused to do anything to help.'

O'Sullivan agrees that the situation could have been sensitive for Australia. She says that the Strides could have been granted 'political asylum', which is a more discretionary act. Other whistleblowers have been granted this in the past, like Swiss-American Christoph Meili, the nightwatchman who disclosed that the Swiss Bank UBS was destroying ledgers that showed the forced sale of Holocaust-era property and, of course, WikiLeaks founder Julian Assange, accused of unlawfully acquiring and publishing thousands of classified US documents who was initially granted asylum by Ecuador.

'Australia could have simply given Mr Stride 'political asylum' but that is rarely done these days,' O'Sullivan says. 'It can be quite a politically sensitive/charged act, as the asylum-granting country is thereby pitting itself against the country that might want the whistleblower back.'

It is hard to deny that Russia is a very powerful and aggressive force; their February 2022 invasion of Ukraine showed that. As a result, most of the rest of the world slapped tougher sanctions on Russia, with Australia's initial tranche including the bank VEB.RF that Shuvalov heads. Further rounds of sanctions have come into effect since then.

Since January 2022, a number of prominent Russians have died in what some commentators have described as strange circumstances, though officially they've been classed as suicide, murder-suicide, a stroke or tragic accidents. These include Leonid Shulman, Igor Nosov, Alexander Tyulakov, Mikhail Watford – a Ukrainian-born Russian oil and gas billionaire found dead in his home in Surrey, England – Vasily Melnikov, Vladislav Avayev, Sergey Protosenya and US businessman Dan Rapoport, an outspoken critic of Putin's war in Ukraine who fell from a high-rise apartment building, and politician and tycoon Pavel Antov, who similarly plunged from a hotel window in India. Twenty-six people, in total, died in 2022 and (at time of writing) fifteen more in 2023 in circumstances that have generally been seen as unusual.

Russian expert Associate Professor William Partlett of Melbourne University says while some of the deaths happened on foreign soil, they were all Russians who perished.

'But it's not irrational for [Nick] to have been concerned and frightened,' Partlett says. 'I completely understand that. Also, the use of fear and intimidation absolutely doesn't surprise me one bit. There's the division, too, between what the state does, and what private interests might do.

'We saw what happened to people like Magnitsky, but I do think that it's less likely the Russian Government would use violence against non-Russian nationals overseas. They have taken action against foreign nationals but only in their own country, as with the arrest of the *Wall Street Journal*'s Evan Gershkovich on charges of espionage. Yet even if the chance of something happening was only one per cent, then just that one per cent could have very significant consequences.'

The ANU's Dr Leonid Petrov believes the dangers are very real. 'New Zealand and Australia aren't considered "friendly" countries to Russia because of their positions on the [Ukraine] war,' he says. 'There can always be sleeper cells and espionage activity revived, having been dormant since the [end of] the War, while the line between the Russian government and the criminal world is now blurred.

'Then there are Russian mafia gangs and hitmen and people like "Putin's Patriots" operating in countries like Australia to back the Kremlin. You have Simeon Boikov, for instance, hiding in the Russian Consulate in Sydney from facing charges relating to the assault of an elderly man. People like him can follow orders and are able to cause trouble for anyone considered an enemy of Putin's regime. They're eager to earn credit from Russia in the hope of being airlifted to Russia in a prisoner exchange. But New Zealand should be safer. It's remote and an island and immigration is tightly controlled.'

So, for the meantime, the family are content just to regroup and rebuild their lives. Nick and Michael are working in the construction industry, building new houses. Their boss, Tom Jenkins, says he enjoys having them on his team. 'They both have a great work ethic,' he says. 'I found them quite reserved when I first met them, but they're a little more relaxed around me now. They've told me just a little of their story. They seem pretty settled.'

Michael enjoys the work as he's now had a lot of experience in construction, and his time on the run turned him into a jack of all trades, with a skill set that means he can now fix virtually anything that's broken, from vehicles to computers, and build whatever else might be needed. He hopes, one day, to set up his own building or carpentry company. 'Even to this day, if I need something fixed, I can quite easily look up how to do it myself,' he says. 'I might get it wrong the first time, but by the second, I'll get it right. It's been ingrained into me from that time.

'The hardest thing for me, coming to live in New Zealand, was getting my driving licence. I'd been driving for years, but always on bush tracks, across sand and swamps and mud, in 4WDs and in manuals, so it was a shock trying to drive a regular vehicle on a proper road. The first few times here, I was hopeless. I had to pull over a few times to get in the right headspace.'

Anya is doing some cleaning work at a nearby hotel, while pursuing her true love: arts and craft. She makes jewellery, she sews, she draws and she dreams of one day meeting someone special, going to live in a log cabin in the country somewhere, and starting her own family. Naturally, she'd take Molly the dog Mark II with her.

'She's grown into a very happy dog,' Anya says. 'She reminds me of myself when I was younger, kind of bright and playful. I'm pretty much good now. But I am tired. I feel like that old lady on her farm who looks out at the sunset at the end of the day and thinks back on all the memories. I feel like my soul is tired.'

Anya ended up having a lot of counselling to help her come to terms with the trauma she suffered as a young girl. Leaving her home, friends and school in Russia overnight at the age of nine, and then being torn away again from everything she knew in Australia to go on the run at age thirteen, as well as the difficulties of fugitive life as a teenager, have left deep scars.

Michael was offered a psychologist, too, but, in typical fashion, decided he'd prefer a DIY solution. 'Obviously, counselling would suit some people and prove extremely valuable to them,' he says. 'But I preferred to listen to a variety of podcasts from experts and other people who've gone through hard times to learn about how they coped. That suited me better. I never like to use the word "trauma" because I don't want to play on that. What happened, happened. But it's undeniable that what we experienced has changed us.'

Helping everyone recover is the new person in their lives, a former Russian ballerina turned ballet teacher, who Nick met in

Christchurch in late 2019. He was in a café, heard her Russian accent, and went over to talk to her. He was bemused to discover her name was Ludmila, the same as his ex-wife, although she uses the different shortened form Mila. For her part, Mila was startled to meet a Russian-speaking Englishman on the South Island of New Zealand.

'We soon started meeting every day, and going walking and talking,' says Mila. 'We walked so far! He started telling me a little bit about his story as I think he was nervous he might frighten me away. But, unknown to him, I Googled his name and came across a newspaper article, so when he finally told me everything, I was prepared, much better than he could have imagined.

'But I got to know him as a person first, and knew he was a very good man who is devoted to his children, and a very good father. We moved in together, and then I faced the difficult choice of moving with him and Michael to the North Island and leaving my ballet school. It was a hard decision, but I'm very happy I made it. We lived together through all the difficulties when Anya was still in Australia and we'd get phone calls at 2am and 3am. Now she is here, and I am very happy to get to know her better, and she is recovering well. Michael is a very calm and intelligent person. I feel very much part of the family now.'

Nick fell head over heels for Mila, and both Michael and, later, Anya, gave him their blessing. 'She lived with all our ups and downs, and supported me mentally without a thought for herself,' Nick says. 'She's the kindest person I've ever met. We live now as a family and the kids love her.

'After everything we've been through, we're now in a very happy place.'

Michael agrees. 'It's taken a while to adjust back to civilisation,' he says. 'I know it sounds strange, but I'm kind of glad we went through all that and had those experiences. But I'm also glad that part of my life is finished.'

Anya, too. is coming to terms with the new 'steadiness' of life. 'It's pretty good now,' she says. 'Everything is so much more normal. I like it, and I love being back with my dad and my brother, and Mila is great. You never know what's going to happen in the future, but I feel stronger now about facing it. I think we all do.'

# ACKNOWLEDGEMENTS

FIRST AND FOREMOST, I want to thank my two loyal companions throughout this whole adventure, my son Michael and daughter Anya. Their faith in me never faltered, and my love for them never wavered. Our lives went through a hell of a rollercoaster, but the one constant was that we were always there for each other. Thanks, guys. You're the absolute greatest.

And I wish nothing but the best for Luda, their mother and my former beautiful companion in life.

I'd also like to mention my two children by my first marriage. It's been a source of enormous sadness that we haven't been a part of each other's lives. One day, I hope we can be reunited again.

For this book, I have a huge debt of gratitude to publishers Simon & Schuster for allowing us to tell our story to the world: Emma Nolan, Rosie McDonald, Dan Williams, Anna O'Grady and Gabby Oberman.

Fiona Inglis, who brokered the deal, was also a terrific support all the way through.

Thanks, too, to Sue Williams, for her talent and passion for writing, and her determination to make our story as thrilling in the telling as it was in the living.

I'd like to acknowledge the US journalist Michael Weiss, as well, for his bravery and dedication to his cause of exposing corruption worldwide.

Personally, our family wants to thank the Indigenous peoples of the Dampier Peninsula, Bardi, Bardi-Jawi, Nyul Nyul, the Burrguk Aboriginal Corporation and the Beagle Bay mob for accepting us and allowing us to live in their community.

In addition, I'd like to express our gratitude to all the friends who showed strength and supported us throughout our troubled journey. That's Steve Delane, Gio, Oleg, Pahom, Lodka, Kieren and Tom Jenkins. And a special thanks to Angie and Mark. Without their love and kindness, I could have lost my daughter. And to all the others we can't name in the book: thank you.

There are other thanks due to the experts who've provided their thoughts on our predicament, like expert lawyer Nilesh Nandan, Russian specialists Associate Professor William Partlett of Melbourne University, Associate Professor Matthew Sussex of the Australian National University's Strategic and Defence Studies Centre and the ANU's Dr Leonid Petrov, as well as Maria O'Sullivan, an Associate Professor in the Deakin Law School in Melbourne.

A special shout-out, too, to my partner, Mila, for being just the most loving and caring person I've ever met.

And last but not least on the rollcall, Molly the dog, Mark I, our loyal protector and guardian, the proud owner of the greatest bark on the Dampier Peninsula.

— Nick Stride

# ABOUT THE AUTHOR

SUE WILLIAMS is an award-winning author and journalist. She has written a number of bestselling books, including *Father Bob: The Larrikin Priest*; *Women of the Outback*; *Mean Streets, Kind Heart: The Father Chris Riley Story* and the historical novel *Elizabeth & Elizabeth*.

Sue was born in England and worked in print and television in the UK and New Zealand. She spent many years travelling around the world before falling in love with Australia in 1989. Since settling here, she has written for many of Australia's leading newspapers and magazines.